AF443365

SECURING YOUR HOME

a Consumer Publication

edited by   Edith Rudinger

published by   Consumers' Association
publishers of **Which?**

Consumer publications are
available from Consumers'
Association and from
booksellers. Details are
given at the end of this book.

© Consumers' Association
October 1981

ISBN 0 85202 207 7
and   0 340 27485 9

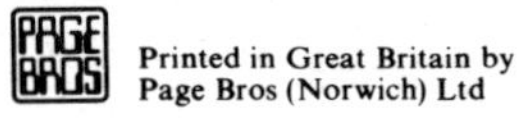

Printed in Great Britain by
Page Bros (Norwich) Ltd

a Consumer Publication

SECURING YOUR HOME

Consumers' Association
publishers of **Which?**
14 Buckingham Street
London WC2N 6DS

CONTENTS

We are continually exhorted by the Home Office, the police, the insurance companies and by the security industry generally to 'Lock up your house' and 'Lock up your car' in order to protect property and help to prevent crime. To convince us of the seriousness of the situation and the need to take action ourselves, they all quote crime figures of one sort or another. But most people cannot relate such numbers to themselves.

To the questions 'What are the chances of my home being burgled?' and 'What are the chances of my car being stolen?', the answer is 'pretty high' – too high for peace of mind or for a complacent attitude towards security. And if you live in one of the big towns or cities, such as London, Birmingham, Manchester, Liverpool and many others with a higher crime rate than most small country towns and villages, the likelihood of being burgled is much greater. This, however, does not imply that if you live in a small town or village you will be immune – far from it.

If your home is burgled, there is a somewhat less than 1 in 3 chance of the burglar being arrested and a minimal chance of your getting your property back.

Before looking at the various means of securing homes and cars, there are a couple of enduring myths about security that have to be dispelled.

Myth no 1 says:
no one will break into my house because I have nothing worth stealing.

That is wrong on two counts: firstly, a burglar is unlikely to know whether you have anything worth stealing until he has broken in to find out and probably caused some damage doing so. (If you have not, he may well vandalise your home out of spite.) Secondly, the majority of people do have quite a lot of easily disposable items of property, which are valuable enough for a burglar to steal. These include TV set, video recorder, hi-fi equipment, transistor radios and radio alarms, cassette player, TV games, cameras, watches, guitar or other musical instrument, electrical kitchen equipment (food processor, coffee maker, toaster and suchlike), electric tools. Many houses also contain some silver, jewellery, clocks, a fur coat (even your suede jacket has quite a good resale value), and most homes have cash and drinks.

Myth no 2 says:
if someone wants to break into my house, there is no way to stop him.

There is an element of truth in this but, in practical terms, a very small element. A skilled burglar will break into almost any premises provided he or she has a good enough motive, a reasonable opportunity and sufficient time. About 85 per cent of all burglaries are committed by opportunists, people who go around looking for easy opportunities to get into someone else's house, steal whatever they can lay their hands on and get out again, quickly, before they are discovered.

Because they are not skilled breakers-in, opportunists look for the easy way in: for example, through a door left on the latch while the occupier pops round the corner to the shop, thinking that she will only be a couple of minutes and that it is not worth while locking up. Unfortunately, that is usually quite long enough for your opportunist. Easy ways in are a door secured by only a simple night latch, windows left open for pets or for ventilation and not locked, windows secured only by a catch; key left in the lock.

Relatively simple and inexpensive security measures will deter these individuals and cause them to go away and try their luck elsewhere.

Skilled, professional burglars are much more difficult to keep out. Professionals tend to attack only those houses where they have found out that the haul will be good enough to make it worth their while, or where they are after specific items that they know are there. They rarely commit what might be termed speculative burglary.

Myth no 3 says:
it does not matter if I am burgled, because I'm insured.

This is not really a myth but the result of slightly illogical thinking. It is fine, provided that your possessions are insured to their full value (many people are under-insured) and that your policy covers any damage caused to the fabric of your home. However, being insured will not bring back things of sentimental value to you or your family. And no amount of money can allay the sense of outrage, shock and revulsion experienced when you find your home and intimate possessions violated by a stranger. Nor will insurance compensate you for the time and trouble involved in clearing up the mess when your home has been vandalised, even if the money will pay for repair of the damage.

You may also find that your insurers, before they will reinsure you after having paid out following a break-in, will demand that you install a much higher degree of security in your home than would have been necessary to keep out the burglars in the first place.

Neglecting security and relying on insurance compensation is not only illogical but shortsighted and socially irresponsible. The more claims insurers have to pay out, the higher the premiums become.

The British Insurance Association has issued a leaflet *No place like home – for thieves*, giving basic precautions to take, with a check list for identifying valuable items of property. The leaflet is available free (send stamped self-addressed envelope) from the BIA at Aldermary House, Queen Street, London EC4N 1TU. The Home Office has published a booklet *Protect your home*, based on the experience of police forces throughout the country, giving suggestions for anti-theft devices and precautions to safeguard your property, including your car. The booklet is available free from police stations, and may be at citizens advice bureaux and libraries.

what does security entail?
A home cannot be 100 per cent secure if you want to keep it pleasant to live in and not resembling a prison. What security does is to buy time: the time it will take a burglar to overcome your security devices – and time is the one thing he does not have. The better your security measures, therefore, the longer it will take him to overcome

them and the longer he will be exposed to the risk of discovery. This, in itself, is a great deterrent.

No security devices, whether they be locks, alarms, safes, gadgets, lights will do any good if they are not used. Having gone to the trouble and expense of installing a good security system that is adequate for your requirements, you must make sure that it is used, regularly and without fail. Younger members of the household may need instructions and periodic reminding about security and being careful with keys.

You and your family will have to exert a certain amount of self-discipline and accept a certain amount of inconvenience in your daily life. All systems and devices vary in their ease of use. Try to install the simplest effective system and do not go for methods that are so fiddley or complicated that you will not always use them.

how much security?
Security for a home includes
- thief resistant locks on all external doors
- locks on all accessible windows
- grilles or bars across windows and the glazed parts of doors
- a burglar alarm system
- a safe.

Which and how much of this you apply to your home depends on the value of your possessions, the area in which you live, and the amount you are prepared to spend. (In some cases, there is no choice because your insurers tell you what you have to do.)

The degree of isolation in which your home stands is relevant. Risk factors are the house being screened by walls, hedges, trees, outhouses, or a lot of open space around – for instance, your house backing on to fields, playing fields, park, golf course. Being overlooked by neighbours is an anti-burglar factor.

When making up your mind what protection you need and where you need it, walk round the outside of the house and think like a burglar.

Try to determine the best way to get in, checking every possible means of gaining access such as doors, particularly back or side door, door from the garage or conservatory; windows, particularly ground floor windows, or windows near a drain pipe or near a flat roof; sky-lights, ventilators, prefabricated panels, meter hatch, pet flap.

Recall those occasions when you forgot your keys and had to break into your own house. If you did not find it difficult, pay particular attention to the place and means of getting in – obviously an area of exceptional risk.

You can get advice and assistance on how much security you need and where it should be applied. The people who can help you include:

crime prevention officer
Every police force has specially trained officers who can give advice on all aspects of security. Go to or telephone your local police station to make an appointment for the crime prevention officer to come to your home. He will carry out a security survey inside and outside the house, and give you detailed advice on how to deal with your security risks. His advice to you is free.

He can suggest types, standards and, where appropriate, brands of equipment, and give you a list of security equipment firms in the area but may not recommend any particular firm, leaving you to make the final choice. If you want him to, he will come back to check what you have chosen and how it has been installed.

burglary insurance surveyor
Most insurance companies employ surveyors to visit premises they are asked to insure for high amounts. You can ask your insurers if they will send a burglary surveyor to visit your premises and give you advice. They will not necessarily do so unless the value of your house contents warrants it. The cost of the survey, including travelling, report writing and so on, has to be met out of the premiums the insurers receive, so as a general rule, insurers do not send a surveyor unless the sum insured is high.

independent security consultant
These freelance specialists are a fairly rare breed. For a fee, one will come and advise on the best equipment to use in any particular case. Most consultants' work is done for commercial firms, but they will advise on private households, too, and, if appropriate, devise a security system especially for you, and recommend suppliers and installers capable of carrying out the work.

Some security consultants are ex-police officers; the local crime prevention officer may know one.

British Security Industry Association
The BSIA is the trade association for the security industry, and can be asked for the names and addresses of lock manufacturers, burglar alarm companies, and so on. The address is 68 St James's Street, London SW1A 1PH.

National Supervisory Council for Intruder Alarms
If you require a burglar alarm installed, the NSCIA at St Ives House, St Ives Road, Maidenhead, Berks SL6 1RD will let you have a free list of its approved installers.

burglary prevention specialists
There are companies who specialise in burglary prevention equipment:
locks, grilles, safes, burglar alarms, entry-phone systems. These types
of firm supply a comprehensive range of products with their own brand
name, and will advise you on which of their products you should have,
and may fit them. You may be able to buy the products from a security
centre, locksmith or ironmonger.

locksmiths
Most locksmiths carry a selection of different types and brands of locks
and will send a fitter to advise on and install the locks you choose. The
Master Locksmiths Association can let you have a list of their members
in your area, if you write to 63 Surbiton Road, Kingston upon Thames,
Surrey KT1 2HG.

A locksmith will give useful advice not only about locks but also bars,
grilles and safes; he is likely to recommend stock that he carries. He
may put you in touch with a burglar alarm company (for which he may
act as agent).

your locks

When you identify your locks, look for a maker's name. If a lock is stamped by its maker, it is likely to be of at least reasonable quality. Unnamed locks are suspect.

The British Standard (BS 3621) for thief resistant locks requires that locks passing the various tests should be able to withstand various methods of attack and be resistant to picking, drilling and sawing, and corrosion. Lever locks must have a minimum of 5 levers, and pin tumbler locks must have a minimum of 6 pins. Locks whose design and manufacture comply with the British Standard will have the appropriate number and the maker's name or trademark stamped on them, and if submitted to testing and passed by the BSI, will also bear the Kitemark.

The lock is tested as a complete unit, with the screws and fixings supplied by the manufacturer; a box staple for a mortise lock must conform to the standard, too. Using shorter screws or weaker fixings would reduce the physical security and render the lock below standard.

The more levers or pins, the more key-secure the lock. The steps cut into the bit of a shank key, or the serrations on a flat key, may not give a true indication. (For instance, the key for a 4 lever lock has five steps on its edge. The face plate on a mortise lock should tell you how many levers are in the lock.

Increased key-security of a lock by an increased number of levers or pins does not necessarily mean increased physical security. Locks of adequate physical security are available which would not meet the BS 3621 in terms of key-security.

The bolt in a lock is generally made of brass (which is not susceptible to rust). But brass is a relatively soft metal and could be sawn through. A good security lock has two hardened steel rods running through the length of the bolt, or has ceramic laminations, which cannot easily be sawn through.

Do not expect a good security lock to be cheap. The ones reported on in *Handyman Which?* February 1981 cost up to £43. Generally as important as the type of mechanism is the strength of the metal of which the lock is made, and the strength of its fixing.

inspecting your locks
Check whether your existing locks are suitable for the security they should be providing and consider also their age and any weaknesses and faults which may make them insecure.

- lock the door
  If the key is hard to turn, see whether the door has dropped. If so, the strain could have worn the key, or the bolt where it rubs on the lock case or where it enters the staple. A worn lock is best regarded as scrap.

- with the door open, turn the lock and remove the key
  Can you push the bolt back? If so, the lock needs replacing. If only the key is worn, you might be able to have the lock re-keyed. (Ask a locksmith to advise you whether it is worth doing so or if the lock is so worn that it should be replaced.)

- for an automatic deadlock, check that the smaller secondary bolt does not enter the staple
  If it does, the deadlocking action will not work. Now depress the smaller bolt and check that you cannot push the main bolt back. If the inside knob should be locked by a reverse turn of the key, check that this does lock it.

- in a cylinder lock, check that you cannot withdraw the key until the cylinder is in the locked position – if you can, the cylinder must be changed
  A keyhole slightly off the upright position is another indication of a worn cylinder.
  It is possible to re-key a cylinder; but unless it is a special type, it is probably as cheap to buy a new one.

- if a lock needs 'fiddling' to operate, remove it and take it to a locksmith to check and, if necessary, replace. (It will be cheaper than having to call him out to let you in.)

If you want to change your lock, there may be no need to fix a complete new lock. With a lever mechanism, only the levers may need to be changed, with a pin tumbler mechanism, only a new cylinder may be needed. In each case, you will get a new set of keys.

Locks need very little in the way of maintenance provided they are correctly fitted and correctly used.

Locks may be lubricated with powdered graphite (obtainable from locksmiths); never use oil.

When you are cleaning around the outside of a lock, make sure that dust, dirt or other matter does not get forced into the mechanism through the keyhole. For instance, if you metal-polish the lock enthusiastically, the pins may end up working in a fine grinding paste.

When painting a door to which a lock is fitted, it is best if the lock is removed so that paint does not get into the mechanism. When the lock is removed, take the opportunity of blowing out any dust which has got into it.

what the burglar tries to do

Some methods of attacking a lock, and some means of countering them, are:

pin tumbler rim locks
- *breaking glass or panel on door, inserting hand and turning knob*
  lock on which internal knob can be locked off so that knob can only be released by key

- *inserting a piece of flexible steel or plastic between the door and the frame and pushing back the bolt*
  deadlockable latch

- *drilling through the keyway to drill out the pins*
  lock with a hardened steel face plate and hardened steel pins

- *picking*
  tumbler lock to BS 3621 has to have an anti-pick device such as 'mushroom' drivers

- *twisting to wrench off the screws holding the cylinder to the lock case*
  chamfered outer ring round the lock to prevent a wrench from gripping

- *force – by barging, jemmying, kicking to fracture the staple or force it out of its fixing*
  more difficult if fixing screws are applied in two directions (with and across the line of force)

mortise lever locks
- *picking*
  lever lock of 8 levers or less to BS 3621 must include some anti-pick device such as false notches on levers and bolt stump

- *drilling to drill out the bolt stump*
  hardened metal plate fitted over the lock case or lock with hardened case

- *jemmying to force back the bolt*
  metal box staple

- *sawing through the bolt*
  hardened steel rods in the bolt head or ceramic laminations

- *trial of keys*
  lock with sufficient differs (the BS demands 1000)

- *skeleton key*
  lock with 5 levers or more.

locks, keys and bolts

Abloy – make of cylinder lock with rotating circular discs; semi-circular key with squared cut-outs on one edge; small semi-circular keyhole

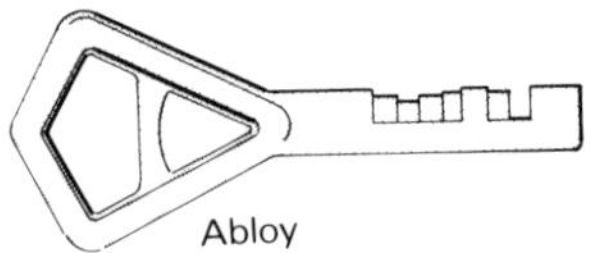

Allen key – not strictly a key, but a hexagonal shaft with right angle bend for operating special screws with hexagonal recess

automatic deadlocking – as bolt enters staple, a small secondary spring-bolt is pushed back by the striking plate, causing a rod to lodge in and immobilise the bolt so that it can only be released by key or knob

Banham's – firm specialising in burglary prevention devices, marketing products of various manufacture under own-brand name

barrel bolt – rounded bar running through guide or holder on door into holder or staple on door frame or wall

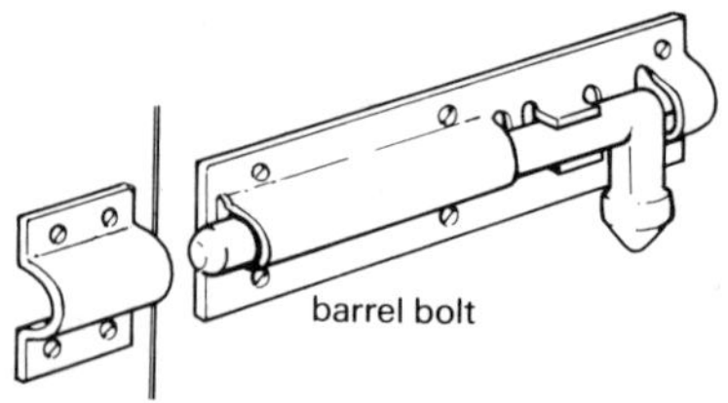

bit – part of key with its edges cut to match the shape of levers or obstructions within the lock so that key fits in and can be turned to move bolt

bolt – metal bar that can be moved across, from the door into the door frame, to hold the door shut

bolt head – the part of the bolt that gets moved out of the casing on or in the door to lodge in the recess (staple) in or on the door frame (BS 3621 requires a deadlocking bolt head to project a minimum of 14 millimetres)

bolt plate – the striking plate

bolt stump – small metal pin in lever type lock; projects from the bolt inside the casing and slots into the cut-outs on each lever

bolt tail – the end of the bolt within the lock

box staple – metal box welded to striking plate to form lining for recess for bolt head in door frame; protects bolt head if door frame chiselled away in attempt to reach and force back the bolt

Bramah – make of special type of cylinder lock mechanism with spring-held steel sliders; pipe key with slots and stump on it

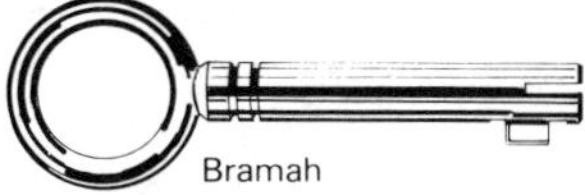
Bramah

Chubb – make of various security devices, including detainer locks of own design with round-stemmed key

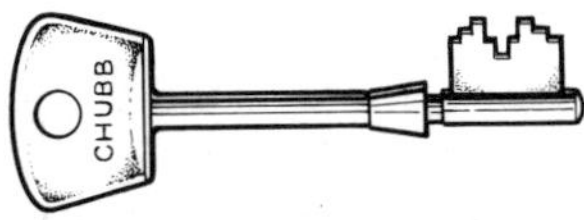

collar – band around shank of key that limits how far it can be inserted into keyhole

connecting bar – in pin tumbler lock, flat metal bar between the cylinder and the mechanism that moves the bolt when turned by key

cylinder – tubular shaped body of lock, with rotating core; generally in rim-fitted lock

deadbolt – bolt in deadlock

deadlock – lock in which the bolt can only be moved out or in by turning with a key (as against a latch bolt, which can be slammed shut)

detainer – in a lever type lock, flat metal plate on a pivot, with a cut-out on the edge. When the detainer is raised by the correct key, the cut-out allows the bolt mechanism to operate

differ – variation in lock mechanism or key profile or shape or size of keyhole or key that enables a lock to be operated by only one key (out of hundreds). Locks conforming to BS 3621 must provide a minimum of 1000 differs, so that 'no lock having the same differ as any other lock is made until at least 999 other locks, each effectively differing from all others, has been made'

disc tumbler lock – lock with similar mechanism to pin tumbler but using a number of flat metal pieces (discs) instead of pins

drivers – top row of pins (of equal length) in tumbler lock, held by springs against pins (of unequal lengths) below

dog bolt – metal projection fitted into edge of door at hinge side, to locate into hole in front frame when door is closed; holds door if hinge sawn through

escutcheon – plate that fits round keyhole; may incorporate flap over hole

espagnolette bolt – vertical bolt running up the height of window or door, activated by handle or lever which simultaneously moves the top half of bolt upwards and bottom half downwards to engage into top and bottom frame

face plate – vertical metal strip; part of lock casing by which lock is fixed into door stile

gate – horizontal of H-shaped cut-out on lever through which bolt stump passes when key raises the levers and moves the bolt

DOG BOLT

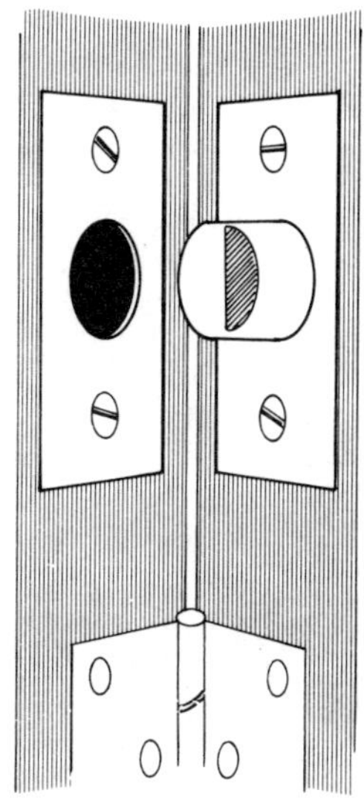

hasp – hinged metal plate with hole at outer end, fitted to door; lodges over staple on the door frame or wall

hinge bolt – dog bolt

hook bolt – bolt with hook-shaped head that latches into staple

Ingersoll – make of various locks, including special type of lever lock with 10 curved levers with notches in different positions; flat key with ridge down its length and serrations on both edges

Kaba – make of cylinder for pin tumbler locks, with rows of pins set horizontally and at an angle; flat key with uncut edges and series of circular indentations along front and back

keep – staple

keyed-to-pass – locks with identical mechanisms, enabling only one key to be used for all

latch – spring-operated bolt, with rounded or bevelled (one sloping edge) head, that can be slammed shut and opened by turning a knob or key; may be deadlockable

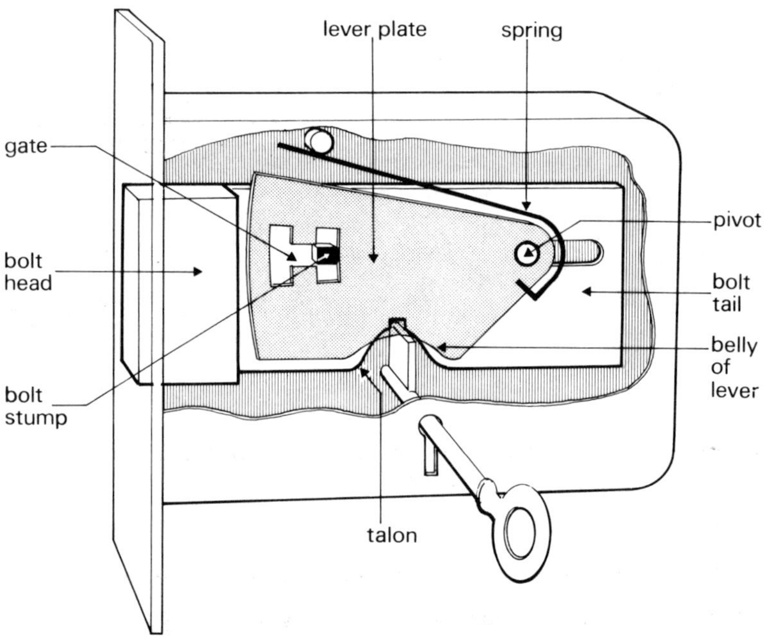

levers – spring-held metal plates inside a lock, each with shape (the belly) cut out along its bottom edge corresponding with the profile of the key and moved by insertion of the key; each lever has H-shaped cut-out in the middle which provides the differs

lever lock – lock whose mechanism consists of a number of metal plates (the levers) placed alongside the bolt, pivoted at one end and held down by a spring. Each plate has an H-shaped cut-out in the centre through which projects a small metal pin (the bolt stump). The position of the gate in each lever is slightly different from that of its neighbour. The key is a round-stemmed shank key with cut-outs in the bit relating to cut-outs in the levers.

When the key is inserted in the lock, it raises the levers so that the horizontal opening of the H (the gate) on each lever is in line with the bolt stump; when the bolt is moved by the key being turned, the bolt stump passes through the gate of all the levers and when the key completes its turn, the levers drop; they are then held down by the action of the spring, trapping the bolt stump in the top upright of the H. No further movement of the bolt can take place until the key is turned in the other direction.

mortise lock – a lock that is embedded in the door so that when the door is shut all that shows is the keyhole on the surface of the door and when it is open the face plate through which the bolt passes on the edge of the door

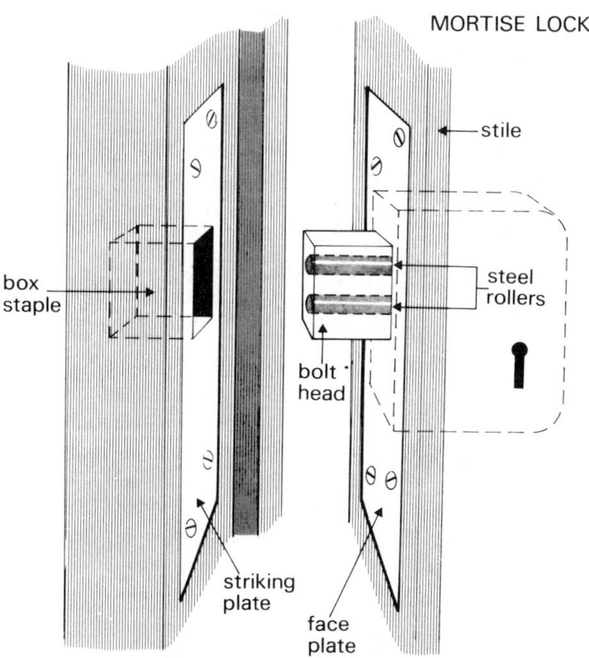

MORTISE RACK BOLT

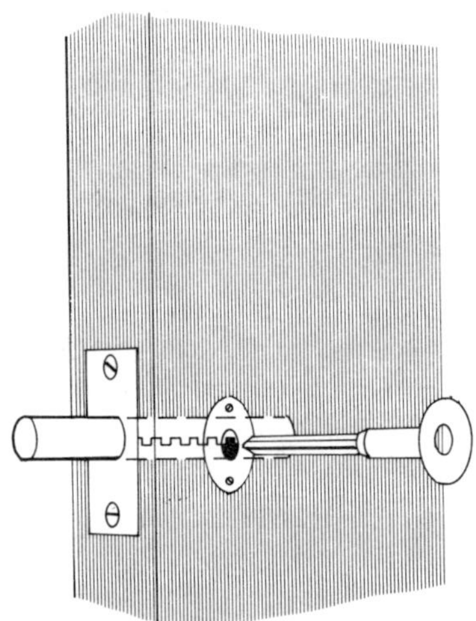

mortise rack bolt – round bolt mortised into door or window with ridges cut inside (the rack) turned by insertion of key with similar ridging which engages with the rack and rolls the bolt across into staple in frame opposite

night latch – lock, generally rim-fitted, with spring bolt operated by a knob or handle on inside and a key on outside; some are deadlockable

padbolt – bolt that can be padlocked on to guide

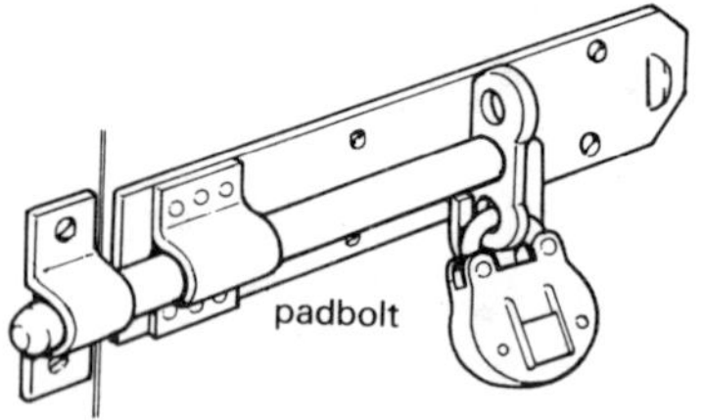

pins – small metal rods in vertical shafts within tumbler lock

pin tumbler lock – cylinder lock with circular core into which the key is inserted and rotated. In the body of the lock is a series of shafts, each containing a spring and a metal pin (driver); in the core there are matching holes also containing pins, of differing lengths. The springs above the pins in the cylinder hold each top pin down against the one under it in the core; this closes the gap between cylinder and core so that the core cannot be rotated.

The profile of the key complements the different lengths of the pins in the core so that when the key is inserted it raises these pins which in turn push up the top pins until the gap between each pin in the core and in the cylinder is in line with the gap between core and cylinder: the obstruction is thus removed and the core is free to turn when moved by the key. Fixed to the rear of the core is a connecting bar which moves the bolt as the core rotates. When the key is withdrawn, the pins tumble down again and immobilise the core.

PIN TUMBLER LOCK MECHANISM

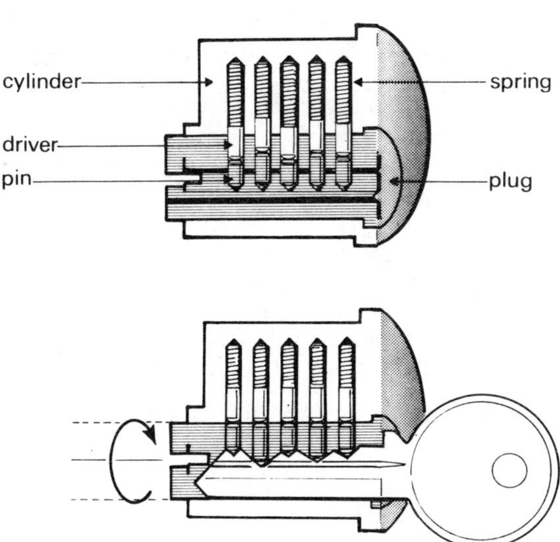

plug – core of cylinder lock that has to be turned for the bolt to move; in locked position, prevented from turning by spring-held pins

rawlbolt – patented expansion bolt; used for fixing into masonry

rim lock or rim latch – lock or latch in casing mounted on inside surface of door; connecting with keyhole on other side of door

NIGHT LATCH

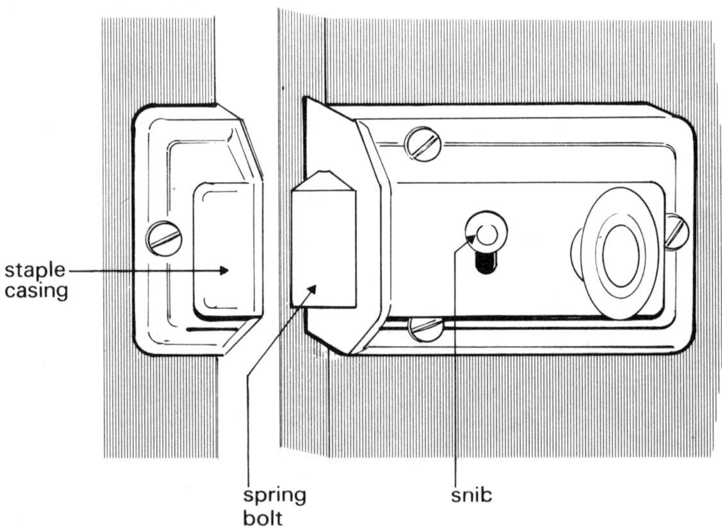

shackle – the hoop of a padlock: a 'close' shackle has minimal space between the hoop and the body of the padlock

shank – the round shaft of key for lever lock

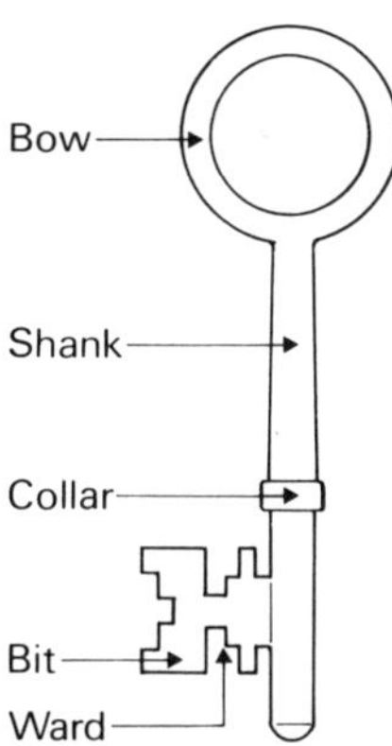

single/double entry – whether key can be inserted in lock from one side of the door only (single) or either side (double)

single/double throw – whether key has to be turned once only (single) or twice (double) to move bolt to maximum projection

skeleton key – key in which the wards have been removed so that it can bypass simple obstructions (wards) in lock

snib – small knob generally on night latches, by which bolt can be held retracted or deadlocked

spring bolt – latch

staple – for mortise lock, recess in door frame to receive bolt; for rim lock, staple is metal case mounted on door frame; for padlock, staple is fixed hoop on door frame or wall over which the hole in the hasp fits and through which the shackle goes

stile – vertical edge of door; its thickness at opening side determines whether a mortise lock can be fitted

striking plate – metal plate fixed to frame of door opposite lock, with hole in it to receive bolt; can incorporate metal box staple

tower bolt – similar to barrel bolt but with two or more short guides instead of one long one

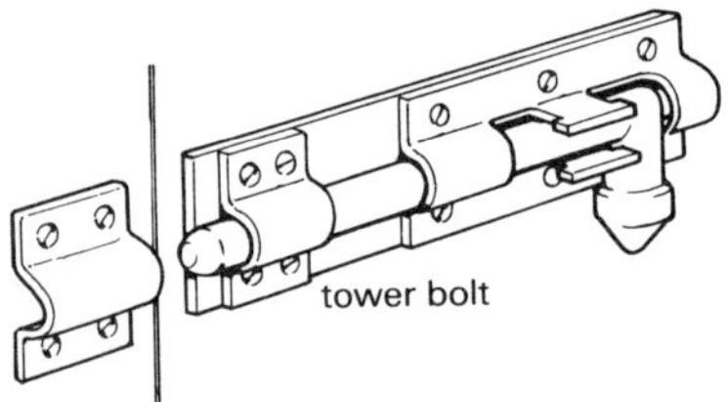

wards – cut-outs on key bit to enable key to pass through correspondingly shaped obstructions (also called wards) within the lock case

Yale – make of various security devices and locks, notably cylinder rim locks with flat key, ridged, serrated along one edge

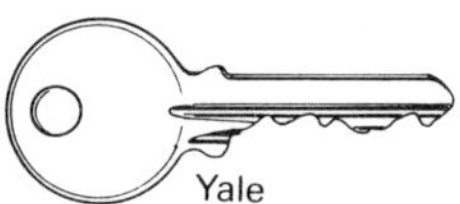

The pin tumber cylinder lock was invented by Linus Yale – and cylinder locks generally tend to be referred to colloquially as 'Yale', even those made by other manufacturers.

The first and most sensible thing to do when starting out on a security programme is to ensure that all your doors and window frames and hinges are in good condition and properly fitting. If they are not, replace, repair or strengthen them as necessary. You will waste both your time and your money if you try to fit good quality locks, or any other security device, to doors or windows that are themselves not very strong, or are in poor condition, badly fitting, or rotting.

Door hinges should be fixed with screws that are as long as the thickness of the door frame or stile will take. A third hinge adds strength – and resistance to brute force – to an inward opening door.

Most locking devices can be improved by stronger and more reliable fixing. If a door is attacked, however strong the hinges, lock and other metal components, it is the screws which are subjected to the force of the impact.

A common weakness of locks, bolts and other security ironmongery is that the screws with which they are supplied are too short or too weak or of the wrong type. A door bolt itself may be strong but the fixing, particularly of the staple, naively weak.

Where there is a risk of tampering, cross-recessed ('Phillips') screws are better than screws with a straight-slotted head. To make the screw irremovable by vandal or burglar, once it is fixed, the recess can be deformed so that it would have to be drilled out to remove.

front door

The front door is usually what is termed the 'final exit door' – that is, the door through which everyone passes when leaving the house to go out to the street. You need to be able to lock it securely from the outside without relying on additional bolts or locks on the inside. Not only the front door, but also the back door or a side door may serve as the final exit door and these must therefore be securely lockable from the outside.

Too many householders rely on a simple 'night latch'. These locks are not, nor were they ever intended to be, security locks.

For strength and security, there should be two locks, one about a third down from the top and the other about a third up from the bottom of the door. It is wasting the locks to fit them too close, too high or too low.

The top lock should be an automatic deadlocking latch. When the door is closed, the latch cannot be forced back by anything inserted between the door and the jamb. With some deadlocking latches, it is possible by a reverse or further turn of the key to secure the inside knob, locking it off so that it cannot be turned. This means that if glass or a panel in the door is broken and a hand inserted, the intruder cannot turn the knob to release the bolt. (Nor can a lawful occupier who is inadvertently locked in.)

For a flat, the BS code of practice for the design of buildings includes in its recommended precautions against fire for flats in a building over two storeys that the door should be fitted with a lock which can be opened by handle from either side and which can only be locked on the outside by key, on the inside by manually operated bolt. This is to avoid the risk of the door being accidentally locked during a fire while one of the occupants is outside raising the alarm.

The bottom lock should preferably be a mortise deadlock, to BS 3621 standard. This lock is to provide extra security when the house is unoccupied. But it will only do so if you do lock it; so do not fall into the habit of not locking the bottom lock when you go out.

In a single-throw lock, the bolt head will project about $\frac{5}{8}$ of an inch into the staple; a double-throw projects farther – but only if the key is turned twice. So, again, it is no good unless you use it properly (particularly as turning the key only once in a double-throw lock may not project the bolt as far as a single-throw mechanism would).

If the door stile is less than $1\frac{3}{4}$ in thick, there would not be enough thickness of wood to take a mortise lock. But a door less than $1\frac{3}{4}$ in thick is in any case not strong enough as a final exit door.

Cutting a mortise in a door weakens the door. You may need to fit metal strengthening plates, incorporating the keyhole, each side of the door round the mortise lock (even though this tends to look unsightly). It is not enough to strengthen the door only at the mortise. The wooden door frame should be strengthened as well where the staple is, by fitting angle iron from the outside, rawlbolted into the surrounding wall.

If a front door is fully or partly glazed, you should replace it with a solid one, or fit grilles over the glazed parts. Ideally, grilles should also be fitted over any adjacent glazing; for example, glass panels beside or above the door. It is not necessary to fit grilles that make the house look like a prison. Diamond-pattern grilles can look reasonably attractive and will prevent a hand being inserted. For a non-standard size door or panel, you may need to have a grille made to measure. An alternative is to fix a sheet of polycarbonate behind the glazed area. This substance is transparent and virtually unbreakable. If an intruder breaks the outer glass, he will be frustrated by the inner lining.

Where the letterbox is just a slit with a flap, a fine mesh wire basket on the door to prevent the mail falling all over the floor also prevents a hand inserted through the letterbox from reaching the lock, or an implement pushed through from getting the key out. A spring on the letterbox flap makes fiddling through it more difficult.

door strength

A *Handyman Which?* report dealing with door strength says that "The construction of a door affects its strength. Generally,
- hardwood is better than softwood, and solid wood doors are stronger than panelled. Given the same stile thickness, wood panelled doors are better than glazed panels but a glazed panelled door with 2 in thick stiles may be more secure than a wood panelled door with thin

stiles (under $1\frac{3}{4}$ in) – particularly if the panels are rebated or plywood.

- framed, ledged and braced doors (tongue-and-groove matchboard with horizontal, vertical and perhaps diagonal bracing) are less secure than most panelled doors.

- flush doors are mostly not strong enough for use as external doors. To find out if yours is a hollow flush door, tap it. If you have (or suspect you have) a weak final exit door and cannot change it, you may need to fit a grille or metal panels over it."

Any wooden door can be strengthened by fixing a steel sheet not less than $\frac{1}{16}$ in thick to the outside face, secured by coach bolts through the thickness (with the nuts inside). There are some multi-locking systems, incorporating vertical bolts and rods, designed to reinforce the door.

It is not much good having strong doors and locks if the door frame will fail under attack. A vulnerable frame can be additionally fixed to the wall with rawlbolts.

There are some firms who produce special security doors which incorporate a steel sheet, behind which the locks are fitted, and which require specially fitted door frames. They are usually produced as a unit, made to measure. Such a door can be given a finish to match that which it is replacing, so that it does not appear to be a special security door. Having such a door may seem extreme but where the property to be protected is very valuable and the risk great, you may consider the trouble and expense justified.

door viewers and chains

A solid door is a good security door, but when the bell rings, you are unable to see who is outside unless you open up. By fitting a door viewer, you can find out who is outside before you open the door. Door viewers are a small tube containing one-way panoramic lenses through which you can look out but an outsider cannot look in (and if the door viewer has a flap, whoever is outside cannot even see if the light is on). Door viewers have different angles of vision; choose one with a wide angle (say, 180°). The length of the viewer should be the thickness of the door. Fix it through a hole drilled into the door at the eyelevel height of the shortest adult in the household. It is advisable to have a light over the door outside which you can switch on from the inside to see who is there.

The occasion will inevitably arise when the doorbell rings, you look out and do not recognise the caller. You should ask who he is and what he wants before letting him in. A chain that lets you open the door just enough to see and speak to the person outside can be fitted. A door chain is usually about 6 in to 8 in long and is fitted to the door frame, and either runs through a metal ring on the door itself or latches into a groove fitted on to the door. The position and the length of the chain and of the holding groove are important, to make sure that the person on the outside cannot reach a hand through the gap to release the chain.

To open the door fully, it is necessary first to close the door to release the chain – which gives you the opportunity to shut the door and leave it that way if you do not wish the person to enter.

It is not much good fitting a door chain to a door that has its opening edge adjacent to a wall, because you would not be able to use it effectively to see the person outside.

Any force applied to the door places the screws which hold the chain on the frame in direct line of force. So, buy a strong chain, not just one made of thin metal alloy, and use long screws for the chain and groove fixing, not just $\frac{1}{2}$ in ones (the screws that come with the chain may be too short).

You can get a chain unit with a key-operated lock. This is useful as a door chain but should not be considered a substitute for a security lock.

When children in the household are ever left alone or allowed to open the door to strangers, they should be well instructed when and how to use the door chain.

With a flat, it is important that the communal front door leading to the street is securely locked as well as the front door to the flat. A door 'phone or intercom and remote control system for unlocking the street door saves having to trail to that door whenever the bell rings, and makes it possible to keep out an unwanted caller. Do not buzz open the door for anyone you do not know or are not expecting, nor for a visitor to any other flat.

other external doors

The security of all the external doors should be equal. There is little sense in fitting strong good quality locks to the front door and leaving the back and side door with a cheap, old lock of dubious security value, perhaps augmented by an elderly bolt. Thieves prefer to attempt to make an entry at the side or rear of a house where they are out of sight.

A cylinder rim latch is simple and convenient for a side or back door when the house is occupied and people keep going out and in. It should be one that can be deadlocked. Unlike the final exit door, these doors can be securable from the inside for locking up when the house is going to be left empty. The doors should have two key-operated mortise rack bolts, or two strong barrel bolts or tower bolts, one near the top and one near the bottom of the door.

On any external door that opens outwards, the hinges are exposed on the outside and so could be cut or filed, or the hinge pin knocked out so that the door can then be forced open on the hinge side. To protect such doors from this sort of attack, hinge bolts (dog bolts) should be fitted about a third of the way down from the top and about a third of the way up from the bottom of the door on the hinge side. The metal projection of the dog bolt engages in the cut-out in the door frame when the door is closed so that even if the hinges are successfully attacked, the dog bolts hold the door on that side.

Dog bolts are particularly important on outward-opening doors, but you should consider fitting them to all doors because burglars may attack the hinges if they see security locks on a door.

sliding doors
Where an external door is a sliding door – for instance, to a sun lounge or patio – it should be secured by a lock with a hook bolt or claw bolt in which the hook clutches the door to the frame, and a second bolt which prevents the door from being lifted to disengage the hook.

An alternative is to fit a security hasp and staple, and padlock the door (but this may not be possible with an aluminium-frame door).

french doors
Glazed double doors known as 'french windows', normally at the rear and giving access to the garden, but sometimes on an upper floor giving on to a balcony, need to be treated as doors from the security point of view. An espagnolette bolt should be fitted up the length of the door which is the second one to be closed, to engage in the top and bottom of the window frame. Mortise rack bolts (the size for doors, not windows) can be fitted on french doors to provide some extra security – but french doors are inevitably a weak point unless grilled or barred.

Windows

All windows that are accessible by any means must be protected, irrespective of which floor they are on, and garage and shed windows, too.

Burglars rarely break glass in a window in order to climb in through the hole because of the risk of injuring themselves on the shards of broken glass. The incidence of deliberate breakage is higher for small panes than large sheets. There appears to be some reluctance on the part of intruders (and vandals) to smash a big sheet of glass and less hesitation about knocking in a small panel.

If burglars do break glass (and they usually prefer not to because of the noise), it is normally in order to insert their hand and open the catch, so that they can climb in through the opened window. Where window locks are fitted, they make the task of the burglar much more difficult because he then has either to force the lock or to break the window. If the windows are further protected by grilles or bars, it is doubtful if he will even try.

Look around your house and consider each openable window: how often is it opened? If the answer is 'never' or 'hardly ever', remove the latch, catch, stay, or other fastening and screw up the window permanently – one security risk less.

window locks

To match the many different types of window designs, a number of different types of window locks have been developed: locks that have conventional lever or pin tumbler mechanisms, locks with a simple screw-up action operated by a special key; locks that secure the opening frame to the fixed frame; locks that provide a stop under the window catch; locks incorporated in the window latch; locks that lock the stay on to its pin; locks that block the channel of sliding windows.

The report in *Handyman Which?* February 1981 reported on locks for windows, and listed brands then available, with price and comparative security rating, for the following types of lock:

window locks
for casement and fanlight (transom) windows

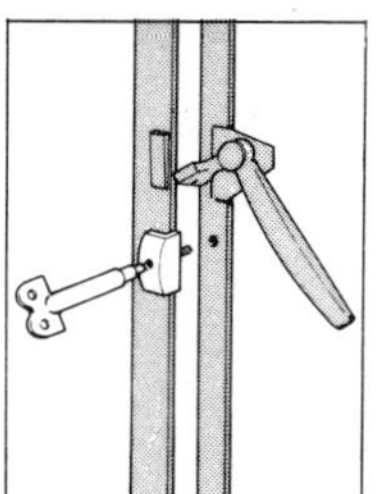

casement lock
locks casement
or fanlight to
frame (models
for both metal
and wood
frames)

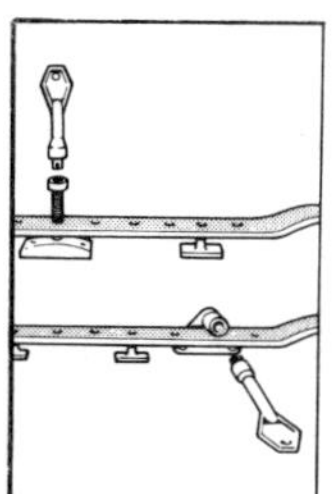

**screw/stop for
casement stay**
prevents
casement or
fanlight stay
being lifted
(models for both
metal and wood
frames)

cockspur stop
prevents handle
on metal
casement
windows being
lifted

dual screw
screws wooden
casement or
fanlight window
to frame

locking bolt
locks casement
or fanlight
window to frame
(models for
metal and
wood frames)

mortise rack bolt
locks wooden
window to frame

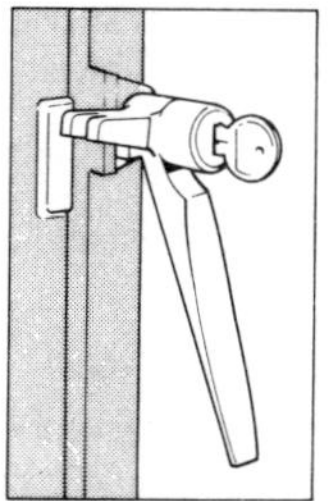

substitute catch
replaces
cockspur handle
on wooden
windows

for sliding sash windows

acorn stop
restricts
movement of
wooden sashes

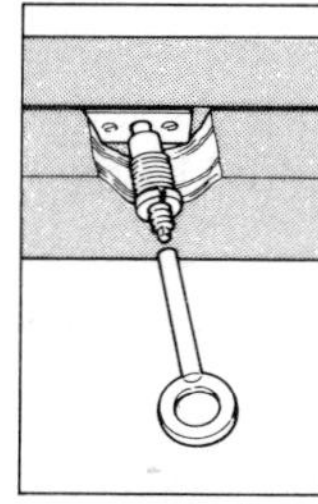

dual screw
screws wooden
sashes together

sash lock
restricts
movement of
sliding sashes –
usually wooden

**sliding window
lock**
restricts
movement of
sliding sashes –
usually metal

Generally speaking, window locks are in themselves quite weak, but properly fitted to a window, they strengthen its security considerably and make it extremely difficult to force from the outside.

Some locks allow the window to be slightly open for ventilation: for example, in a casement window, locking the stay on to its pin in either the closed or a slightly open position; in a sash window, a dual screw which locks the top sash either tight shut or a few inches open. But if the window, although secured, is in a sufficiently open position to let a hand or instrument be inserted to get at the lock on the inside, security is negated.

A wide range of window locking devices is available in hardware shops and department stores, as well as specialist outlets. Because of the variations between the various types of window, not all locks are suitable for any one particular type of window. Also, the shape, width and thickness of the frame of one make of window may preclude the use of a lock which is suitable for a similar type of window of a different make.

The type of lock that you select will be dictated in part by which of the available locks will suit the windows in your house and in part by your own preference for the appearance and method of operation of those that do.

There is little point in trying to fit a window lock to a window in poor condition: badly fitting, warped or rusty or one with a weak catch. Nor is there any point in having window locks if you do not do them up when you are out, or at night.

Some types of window present specific difficulties.

aluminium replacement windows
Over the past few years, many people have replaced existing windows with new aluminium windows which are rot-resistant and do not require painting. Generally, the locking devices fitted as standard provide poor

security, and due to the thinness of the aluminium frames, it is difficult to fit any of the standard window locks successfully.

It is, however, possible to get locks of the screw-up variety specially adapted for aluminium windows. For side-hung casements, or top-hung windows, the opening frame can be secured to the fixed frame; for sliding windows, there are devices to lock the moving frame into the channel. What lock can be used depends on the thickness of the aluminium frame.

louvre windows

Louvre windows should not be installed where they offer access to the house from the outside. An intruder can all too easily slip out the glass, making no noise in the process, and insert a hand and open up the louvres. The remaining blades can then be slid easily from their horizontal position.

It is possible to improve the security of louvres a little by sticking the glass blades to the bladeholders by an epoxy resin adhesive.

Louvre windows are now available with the glass blades fixed into the holders or can have a plastic blade-locking device that is stuck to the glass and the bladeholder on the inside.

Even if you have the special louvres or have glued your ordinary type, they remain a security risk, so you should fit either grilles or bars over the windows on the inside.

ventilators

A ventilator is essential for the safe operation of some gas-fired equipment. Ventilators are often located in glazed areas or near to open windows and some are easily removed from the outside, giving access to the window latch. This latch should, therefore, have a lock. But before installing any ventilator, think of the security factor of the location.

plastic frame windows
Like aluminium windows, plastic frames do not need painting and do not rot. But they are very difficult or impossible to secure. Their catches are generally of poor quality from the security point of view and it is impossible to fit standard window locks to frames constructed of plastic. So, to achieve security, grilles or bars have to be fitted over them on the inside.

secondary glazing
Double-glazing which consists of two sets of panes improves security a little bit, but only if the secondary panes are themselves capable of being secured. Some manufacturers supply secondary glazing already fitted with security locks. Even so, the frames tend to be flimsy so that for security, window locks should be fitted to the primary (outer) windows.

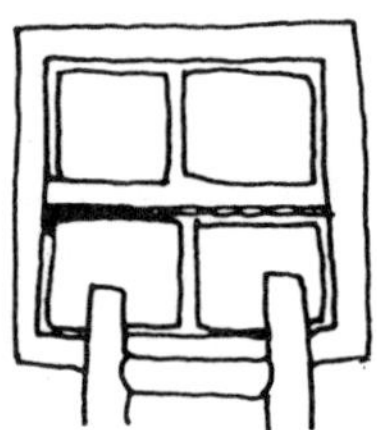

general security
While ground floor windows, and particularly those out of sight of neighbours or passers-by, are most favoured by burglars, it is not much good fitting window locking devices on selected windows only: every window that can be reached from the ground, drain pipe, roof, tree, adjoining wall, is vulnerable. And do not forget to make sky-lights securely lockable – and to lock them. Always close the windows when the house is left empty, not fotgetting bathroom and lavatory windows (generally a drainpipe is near).

The glass pane in a wooden window is commonly fixed with putty. When first applied, putty is very soft and takes up to a year to harden fully. During the hardening time the pane might be easily removable. After some years, it tends to harden to such an extent that it flakes off or large pieces fall out; at that stage, the pane might again be easily removable.

Handyman Which? reported on windows and patio doors in August 1981, including the safety aspects of toughened and laminated glass.

The type of glass pane with wire mesh embedded in it has little security value, making a very quick break-in – say, to open the door latch – only slightly more difficult.

Leaded glass, such as is in stained glass windows, is very vulnerable and even if wired to an internal cross-rod is not strong enough to offer security.

Glazing at below waist level is vulnerable to being kicked in and climbed through, so should be replaced or protected as a priority.

grilles

Additional security for glazed areas, such as accessible windows and sky-lights, is to have a made-to-measure grille or bars over them. A locksmith can be asked about making, supplying and installing. If you tell the smith what you want the grille for, he will spot-weld the touching parts and then mask (and so reinforce) the welds with a decorative rosette or a button.

The visual effect of a grille can be lightened without loss of strength by the metal being worked edge on to the eye, not flat on, and by finishing it with a white eggshell matt paint. Tipping the features of the pattern here and there with a little touch of gold paint also relieves the appearance. Do not go for long sweeping open diagonal or vertical designs, which can be easily prised apart.

A security grille is generally of an elongated diamond pattern constructed of expanded metal mesh. The dimension of the 'diamond' (for example, $1\frac{1}{2}$ in × 3 in, or 7 in × 3 in, or $1\frac{1}{2}$ in × $\frac{3}{4}$ in) would depend on the size of the pane to be protected. The mesh should be welded to a flat steel frame and fixed internally to the window frame with screws at least $1\frac{1}{2}$ in long, about 10 in apart, or rawlbolted into the brickwork round the window. These fixed grilles are a hindrance when you want to clean the windows.

An alternative is to have hinged grille frames with the swinging end of the grille secured by a padlock through a staple fixed to the window frame or wall. Or the grille could be secured by drop pins through hasp and staple at top, middle and bottom (one perhaps padlocked).

Decorative scrolled grilles do not give quite the same degree of protection as mesh grilles but they are adequate to deter the opportunist burglar and they are more pleasant to live with. They also should be welded to flat metal frames fitted to the window frame by screws or rawlbolted to the wall, or hinged.

Where panes of glass are too small for a person to climb through, a fixed grille could be fitted to run parallel with the glazing bars so that the grille is unobtrusive. Where the panes of glass are larger, a grille made up into something like 8 in squares can when a net curtain is drawn across the window inside look like small panes of glass.

bars

Bars are an even more permanent fixture than grilles. They are made of mild steel and can be square or round; they should not be less than about $\frac{5}{8}$ in section or diameter. The distance between the centre of one bar and the centre of the next one should not be more than 5 in. If over 2 ft long, the bars should have a tie bar halfway along their length; if over 4 ft long, a tie bar every 2 ft up. Each bar should be welded to the tie bar to strengthen them against attempts to bend them apart.

If installed externally, the ends of the bars should be grouted about 3 in deep into the brickwork surrounding the window. If internally installed, they should be welded to a flat metal frame the size of the window recess, and the frame rawlbolted into the brickwork of the recess.

telescopic gates

There are sliding folding grilles (like the doors of an old-fashioned lift) which can be fitted on the inside as a protection across a large glazed area, such as french windows. They are considerably more expensive than fixed grilles but have the advantage that they can be pushed back while you are at home so that you do not have to look out of your windows through a grille.

External security

Placing as many obstacles as possible in his way makes the burglar's life difficult and forces him to do things that are going to bring him to notice before he can even begin to break in. The opportunist usually becomes discouraged at a very early stage and goes away to try his luck elsewhere; the professional may well be spotted and reported while still in the preliminary stages of his work.

Ways of access at the rear and side of premises should be protected, as part of the overall design of making the life of the burglar harder. If the side gate is open, he can slip quietly through and go round to the back of the house, out of sight. Otherwise, he would have to climb over and become immediately conspicuous – something burglars try to avoid.

Doors giving access to the side or rear of the premises and to a basement area should be fitted with a security lock or padlock.

A ladder always presents a security problem, particularly one that is too long to be stored in the garage or shed. Where the ladder must be kept outside, it should be secured with chain and padlock against something substantial – the wall of the house itself or the garden wall if you have one. Brackets on which to hang a ladder, having a hinged top bar which padlocks over the ladder side member, are obtainable.

garage and shed

The average garage is a veritable treasure house of tools, tools that are not only expensive to replace if stolen but which can be utilised as housebreaking implements, saving the burglar the trouble of bringing his own with him. The same thing applies to garden sheds or an outhouse; some garden tools make perfect breaking-in implements. (Encourage your next door neighbours to keep theirs locked up, too.)

Garage and shed windows should be protected by grilles fitted on the inside. An alternative is to reglaze with translucent glass reinforced plastic (GRP) or polycarbonate sheets.

In addition to the ordinary lock in a shed door, fit a padbolt or, better still, a security hasp and staple for use with a close shackle padlock.

A security padlock for external use should have a minimum of 5 levers or pins and should be of the 'close shackle' type, so that when the padlock is fitted through the hasp, the shackle cannot be wrenched apart. Padlock, shackle and hasp should be of hardened metal so that they cannot be sawn through. If the lock is for use out of doors, it should be one with a flap over the keyhole.

A security hasp and staple is the type in which, when closed over, the hasp conceals the fixing screws of both hasp and staple, or the type that is bolted on by coach bolts. Screws should be of adequate size and length so that the hasp or staple cannot be prised off with a jemmy.

For external joinery, use rustproof wood-screws, such as zinc-plated, chrome-plated or brass. Plain steel screws tend to rust and then become loose and insecure, especially under strain.

If a garage has double doors, the first closing door must be secured by heavy duty barrel bolts on the inside at the top and bottom, the top bolt shooting into the door frame and the bottom into a socket in the floor. Remember to keep the socket clear of dust and dirt so that the bolt can always shoot right home. The second closing door should have a security lock (such as a deadlockable rim latch, or a mortise lock if the door is thick enough to take it).

An up-and-over door, particularly one that does not have a locking handle, and also a roll-down door, should have a staple bolted on to the bottom and a hasp grouted or rawlbolted into the concrete floor, and be secured by a heavy duty, close shackle padlock with a flap over the keyhole. Where the door surround allows, locking bolts can be fitted on the left hand and right hand side of the door, operated by a key from the outside. Some up-and-over doors are fitted with lock bars on the corners inside, which strengthen the door against forcing.

A side door to a garage should also have a security lock.

Where the garage is built on to the side of the house, forming an integral part, and there is an interconnecting door, a burglar who manages to gain access to the garage can then work away quite happily, out of sight, to break into the house. Such a door should therefore be treated as a final exit door, with an appropriate security lock.

walls
Brick walls are not very effective as a defence because they can be scaled (even the wall at Buckingham Palace). Broken glass cemented on top of a brick wall will be a deterrent to the casual lads, but a determined burglar would neutralise the obstacle with an old sack thrown over to give himself a safe length to straddle.

Anti-climb paint is a thick paint which dries on the outside forming a very thin skin, but remains wet underneath the skin. It is useful for putting on to drain pipes, tops of porches, ground floor extension roofs, tops of walls. As soon as an athletic burglar starts to haul himself up and grasps anything painted with this substance, the pressure breaks the thin skin and he slips on the wet paint underneath.

The paint should be applied carefully and thoroughly, especially to pipes to make sure that the backs of the pipes are liberally coated. It comes in a variety of colours to match in with your external decor. It dries slowly, taking up to 8 hours; dust and insects may get caught on it and trapped as the paint is drying, spoiling the appearance.

Anti-climb paint should only be applied above a height of about 7 ft so that you and your family, friends and lawful visitors cannot accidentally brush against it (warn the window-cleaner, too). It may need to be renewed every 5 years or so.

An alternative protection on a drain pipe leading to, or past, a window would be a collar of angled spikes, or a surround of cement so that there is no handhold around the pipe.

Barbed wire can be used as a defence: coiled along the side gate or strained above a fence or wound around drain pipes at, say, 10 ft up. (The Colditz look can be relieved by training rambling roses over the wire. Clematis can be grown to disguise barbed wire obstacles attached to the house – clematis being too fragile to support a human climber.)

A thick holly or hawthorn hedge, once established (which may take some years) not only guards privacy but can be effectively offputting to an intruder.

illumination

Burglars of whatever degree of competence – opportunist or professional – dislike being seen at work. This is the reason why they tend to work when there are few people about or when darkness masks their activities. So, if your home is illuminated externally, they may not even try to break in after dark.

Bright external lighting should be installed for areas such as over the front door, in front of the garage and near the back door. The lamp unit should be one designed for out-of-doors use.

If the lamp is angled downwards to bathe the wall area in light, anyone working on a door or window would be clearly visible and it would avoid too much light spilling into the neighbours' garden and causing them annoyance.

The lamps should be installed fairly high on the wall to prevent them being easily put out of action, with the cable as inaccessible from the outside as possible. The lamps should be connected to a switch inside the house. The use of a time switch to control the outside lighting ensures that the lights go on when it gets dark even if you are not at home. There is also a switch controlled by the amount of daylight, and not dependent on a time switch. This is useful if you are going away for, say, a month when it will become dark at different times.

Some burglar alarm systems can be connected to external lights, so that if someone breaks in and activates the alarm, the lights come on, calling visible attention to the premises being attacked – but for this to be effective, the light has to be in a conspicuous, unusual position, or flashing.

Look for shadow zones – it may perhaps be worth trimming a tree or bush to throw light into some dark corner.

If the area around the front door is kept free of shrubbery which could provide cover for a thief and is well lit, it helps to prevent the householder being attacked on his own doorstep and his own keys being used to gain entry.

There are some back-up measures to support and supplement your primary security devices. Some of these are illusory in effect for use when you are out, and some concern discipline and practice. These cost nothing. They apply generally to what you do when you are going out, or away on holiday.

keys

Keys should not be tagged with your home address, in case you lose them and they are picked up by a dishonest person. An honest person may hand them over to the police, so you should have some means of identification on the key ring that does not indicate where you live.

If keys are lost, especially if in a lost purse or handbag which contains your name or address or telephone number, notify the police immediately and make sure that the house or flat is constantly occupied (by an able-bodied adult) until either the keys are recovered or the locks, or at least lock mechanisms, have been replaced. Even if the keys are returned, copies may have been made, so it is safest to change the locks immediately.

The more locks you have, the more keys you have to carry around. Where you have several (or only two) locks of the same mechanism and make, they can be 'keyed to pass' – that is, have identical mechanisms that are operated by the same key. If, for example, your house has a front, side and rear door and you fit a mortise lever lock and a cylinder rim latch to each door, the three lever locks can be keyed to pass, and so can the three tumbler locks. You end up with two keys only, to operate all the locks on the external doors of your house.

Some lock manufacturers have an owner-registration scheme: additional keys are supplied only against signature(s) corresponding to the record on the registration card that was filed at the time when the lock was originally bought. Locks with registered design and restricted key blanks are also available: to obtain extra keys, one of the original has to be sent in to the manufacturer, with a letter of authority. Generally,

locksmiths or keycutting shops do not hold the blanks for such keys, so cannot copy them.

where to keep keys
Keys should not be left in the lock of any external door. Thin long-nosed pliers operated from the outside can grip the end of the key in a lever lock and open it. Or the key might be pushed out to drop on to a piece of paper pushed under the door: if the door is not well-fitting at the bottom, paper and key can be pulled to the outside, or the key hooked out with a piece of wire.

Burglars often break in through a window at the rear or side of the house and immediately unlock doors with keys in them, ready for a quick getaway. They can then remove bulky objects, such as a television set, through the door. No keys, therefore, means that the burglar would have to break out forcibly and this would be time consuming and noisy, and dangerous from his point of view.

Do not leave keys under the mat or in a flower tub or other 'secret' place outside – where burglars often find them.

in doors?
When you are in the house, there is the conflict between security from a break-in and ease of getting out in an emergency. There are occasions, fire is the most obvious one, when you may need to make a hurried exit. It may be vital to be able to open the nearest external door, or window if an escape from upstairs is necessary, in the shortest possible time. One solution is to put a key in a position near the door, known to all members of the household but not obvious or accessible to someone who does not know the key is there. The key would have to be used only in case of emergency so that it would otherwise always

be in the same position. (But fire officers do not like this idea much.)

Many people fear that when they are watching TV in the evening, they may not hear someone force the front door, who would then enter and rifle the other rooms. This has happened on numerous occasions so the fear is reasonable. People therefore lock the mortise lock on the front door, and tend then to leave it locked when the family go to bed. While this is excellent practice from the security point of view, it is not advisable on grounds of safety.

There are inexpensive battery-operated devices obtainable, which will give off a piercing whistle when disturbed. One type is a door wedge, which can be pushed gently under the front door: any movement will set off the alarm. Another type can be hooked to a door or window, and the operating pin tied to the frame. Provided the batteries are changed occasionally, these devices can frighten off an intruder and alert inhabitants, even while they are watching TV downstairs or while upstairs using the vacuum cleaner.

Another idea for evening and night security is to have barrel bolts, one at the top and one at the bottom of the external door, and use them when everybody has come home, leaving the mortise lock unlocked. In case of fire, you need only slip the bolts back and turn the knob of the rim latch, and the door will open.

locking internal doors
There are basic arguments for and against locking internal doors. One says that you should lock all your internal doors whenever you are out; then if someone breaks into the house in your absence, he is confined to one room and cannot get into the rest of the house. The other says that you should leave all your internal doors unlocked when you are out; then if someone manages to break in, he will not cause damage breaking into other parts of the house – damage perhaps far in excess of the value of any property stolen.

The choice must depend on individual circumstances. If you leave the internal doors locked when you are out and someone does manage to break in, since there is no one at home to hear if he makes a noise breaking from one part of the house to another, the damage he causes may well be extensive.

But you may prefer to risk the damage to the doors – they can be repaired and the insurance will pay – to reduce the risk of loss of possessions that are not easily replaced. A determined burglar will break down doors, but a casual one will not have the tools and may not want to risk being in the house for long.

When you are home, however, in bed at night, or perhaps watching TV or listening to the radio in the evening when everybody is in one room, you may want to lock all the other internal doors so that if someone does break in and try to pass from one room to another, you will surely hear. But bear in mind fire escape problems of removing keys from locks.

lights
It is quite common for people to leave lights on indoors when they go out in the evening, as a pretence that there is somebody at home. But a hall light left on with the remainder of the house in darkness is rather like hanging up a notice outside saying: 'I'm out – come on in and help yourself'. (And leaving a light burning all evening in the loo is not likely to make him think that there is someone at home.)

Leave the hall light on by all means (it is probably normally left burning all evening, anyway) but also leave a table lamp alight near a front room window, with the curtains drawn so that it looks as though the family is in, watching TV. Or leave a small light burning in a bedroom with the curtains drawn, so that it looks as though someone is reading in bed.

There are several varieties of time switches, which can be pre-set to come on and switch off at various times. So, if you are going to be out all day until late, or you are away for several days, a light can come on in the evening and go off at bedtime. You will have to set the gadget properly to ensure that the lights do not come on in the middle of the afternoon or stay on all night – that would tend to draw the attention of thieves.

There is a light-sensitive switch which turns on the light as it gets dark outside, and switches off a set number of hours later.

Another light-controlling gadget is a random-selection timer. You plug it into the light socket, either hanging from the ceiling or in a reading or a standard lamp, and put the light bulb into it. When you switch on the light, it pleases itself when it comes on, for how long it stays on, and when it switches off.

animals

Some people swear that an animal is the finest and most effective deterrent to burglars there is. A ravenous leopard or tiger might make short shrift of a burglar, but dogs have a somewhat dubious security value. Generally, family pets do not make good guard dogs: they are accustomed to human beings around them generally, and accustomed to strange human beings being introduced into the bosom of the family as guests whom they are discouraged from biting or otherwise seeing off the premises. On the whole, however, burglars are wary of dogs and a yappy pet dog may well deter a casual burglar. But do not rely on Fido.

For a country dweller, geese are traditionally a good alarm system, setting up a great commotion at the slightest deviation from normality.

callers

It is an elementary rule not to let anyone unknown over your threshold, be it a salesperson, a market researcher, a 'man from the council', a political canvasser or religious evangelizer, a door-to-door collector or someone delivering a parcel. Not only might they attack or harm you or themselves steal while your back is turned, but they may be 'casing the joint', reconnoitring in preparation for a return visit by self or accomplice.

Keep the door chain on until you are quite sure.

A bona fide caller will not mind being asked for proof of identity and authority. Look very carefully at whatever proof is offered, and do not be fooled by a uniform, badge or cap. If you are suspicious, check by telephoning the organisation he/she claims to represent – but look up the number in the telephone directory; do not use the number given by the caller.

In many homes, all members of the family are out at work all day, so that when the electricity or gas meter readers call, there is no one to let them in. Sometimes they leave a card and ask you to read the meter yourself and leave the completed card in an obvious place for the meter reader to see (such as in the front ground floor window) or to collect from outside the front door. This tells the world and the burglar that the house is unoccupied. So, despite the request on the card, when you have read the meter, put the card in the post.

An arrangement either between a group of neighbours or between just two, to keep an eye on each other's property during holidays and at other times is difficult to better. Neighbours know each others' routines and should be encouraged to challenge knockers-at-the-door. Do not say to the person standing at your neighbour's door "They're always out all day" or "They won't be home till late" but say "She'll be back soon. Can I take a message?". If the visitor declines the offer, be alerted: take a good look to remember his or her appearance and, after checking with the neighbour, be prepared to report to the police.

At the risk of seeming nosey, neighbours should report to each other any unusual person or event on or around their property. Better be nosey than indifferent. It is not enough to protect your own property; if everybody cared about the security of neighbours, too, they would reciprocate. Cooperation between neighbours may be just as important as locking devices.

Do not assume that the prospective miscreant is invariably a readily recognised suspicious-looking male. Girls are in it, too, and the track-suited female with her sports bag may well be looking for loot.

going on holiday

When you go away, leave the keys to your house or flat with a reliable friend or neighbour. But the keys should not be labelled with your name, let alone the address.

If possible, make arrangements that the friend or neighbour goes in each day, opens windows for ventilation and to give the appearance of occupancy (and closes them again before leaving). Ask him or her to remove not only letters but all the leaflets and other papers and unsolicited rubbish that gets stuck into letterboxes or under doors and, if left, advertises the occupant's absence from home. A length of heavy fabric fixed behind the letter flap prevents anyone peering through or listening whether there are sounds within.

In the summer, the neighbour might be willing to mow the lawn and water the plants, if necessary. In the winter, if it should snow, perhaps he would keep the route to the front or back door clear. (And be prepared to do the same for your neighbours when they go on holiday.)

Give the friend or neighbour your holiday address and a telephone number, if possible, and authorise him or her to notify the police if anything seems suspicious or goes wrong.

Stop the milk and the newspapers and laundry delivery. See the milkman in person rather than leave a note: a note in an empty milk bottle indicates absence.

During the last war, there was a slogan which said 'Careless talk costs lives'; in peacetime, careless talk helps thieves. Be careful who hears you tell that you are going away. Do not talk about it in the local pub or tell local shopkeepers or the hairdresser unless it is necessary for them to know, because you never know who can overhear what you are saying. Some people like to tell the police that they are going away but, these days, the police do not have the resources to wander around unoccupied houses – and, indeed, when they do so, it could advertise the fact that the premises are unoccupied.

Before leaving, put any clocks that need winding out of sight or hide them. Do not stand all your potted plants in the kitchen sink where a glance through the window will thus reveal your absence. Put valuables out of sight (if you hide them, remember where you put them) and possibly take them out of the home and board them with a friend or at the bank. Lock away gardening tools and, particularly, any ladders.

Make sure you have locked all doors, shut the windows, set any burglar alarm system. Do not leave blinds or curtains drawn across windows. If you go away by car, try not to make the packing-up and departure too obvious. Label your luggage which will be hanging around airports and stations with your holiday destination only and put your home address inside the case. Be suspicious of anyone asking "How long will you be gone for?" If people do not need to know, do not tell them: that is the basis of security.

Apart from securing the holes in your house – that is, the doors and windows – and the security of other areas of the periphery, a second line of defence for your property is warning devices, such as alarms.

A burglar alarm (electric intruder detection system) is an electrically operated system of detection devices linked to a control box, that gives a warning when something is done to activate the detectors. Its function is to announce that someone is breaking in or has broken in, or to scare off the intruder, or both. An alarm does not physically keep anyone out of premises. Its effectiveness is related to the number, positioning and reliability of the detection devices, the effectiveness and reliability of the signalling, and the speed and reliability of the human response to the alarm.

Alarm protection can mean that detection devices are installed at all external doors and all accessible windows, connected to the alarm system; or perhaps only one part of the premises, or placed in a logical sequence where a thief might be expected to move through the house.

Most systems installed by a burglar alarm company run from mains electricity with a re-chargeable battery as a stand-by; some alarms are entirely battery powered (these are mainly the ones for installation by yourself).

You use the control box to switch the system on and off. Some systems have a delay mechanism of a minute or so, to allow you to get out of the house without setting off the alarm when, for instance, you open the front door. And similarly when you re-enter, you have a minute to get to the control box and switch off the whole system before the alarm sounds. Most systems have a remote control (shunt) switch which can be fitted wherever convenient, even outside the house, so that you can switch on and off from there. Some door locks are made to incorporate a microswitch so that when the door is locked, the alarm is set. In some systems there is a bypass switch, so that part of the system can be switched on and off independently of the rest.

In an open circuit system, no electricity flows until the electric circuit is closed by (the intruder's) movements. In a closed circuit system, it is the breaking of the electric circuit which causes the alarm to sound off. If you have the two different types in your alarm system, they need two separate electric circuits: one closed and one open. The wiring should be concealed, and so should be the control box and switches. Do not tell anyone who need not know where they are.

The various devices work in different ways.

Magnetic contacts are small devices in two parts, for use on external doors and accessible windows. One part of the device is set on the door or window, and the other part set into the frame. While the door or window is shut tight, the two parts of the contact are held together and the electrical circuit is complete. If the door or window is opened, the circuit is broken and the system is activated.

A variation of this type is a contact recessed in the door frame and a spring loaded plunger held against it when the door is closed. When the door is opened, the circuit is broken and the alarm is activated.

Other types of device are 'vibration detectors' which are stuck to the window glass. They are activated by the vibrations caused by breaking glass or the removal of the putty. Another similar device is metallic foil carrying an electric current, stuck round the window: if the glass is broken, the foil is also broken, breaking the current and activating the alarm system.

Doors may be fitted with what is known as 'lace and board' protection. This consists of a continuous thin wire, contacted on to the alarm system that is run up and down the door at about two-inch intervals and covered by a sheet of hardboard to protect it against accidental damage. Any attempt to cut through the door breaks the wire and activates the alarm.

There are also detection devices which are tuned to be activated by the sound of glass breaking, and devices that are fitted to walls that pick up the sounds of, and are activated by, the vibrations caused by

someone breaking through the wall. (But they may also be activated by heavy traffic passing.) These types of devices are normally used only in high risk premises.

To give warning of a burglar once he has got inside the house, you can install alarm 'traps' around the house, by fitting magnetic contacts to internal doors. In addition, you can place pressure mats in various strategic places – under the carpet at the foot of the stairs, in front of the TV set, anywhere you feel a burglar might go, such as just inside rear windows.

Pressure mats are 'open circuit' devices. When the mat or pad is squashed – by someone treading on it – the contacts come together, complete the electrical circuit and activate the alarm. The disadvantages of pressure mats or pads are that a false alarm can easily be caused by a visitor (or his dog) stepping on the mat. You have to be careful where you place your furniture in relation to the mats or vice versa. The mats are vulnerable to wear and tear and if you have fitted carpets these have to be taken up when the pressure mats need replacing and are likely not to fit so well again afterwards.

Another form of trap protection is provided by 'volumetric' devices. For instance, infra red rays are projected across an empty space by a transmitter to a receiver and form an invisible barrier. If the ray is broken by someone walking through it, the receiver immediately activates the alarm.

What is known as 'passive' infra red equipment is a receiver unit only. It recognises any change in the ambient level of infra red energy, such as is caused by a person entering or leaving the protected area. This would cause the device to activate the alarm.

'Ultrasonics' and 'microwaves' are other types of space protectors, which protect fairly large areas. They consist of a transmitter which sends out signals in a certain pattern, which, if received by the receiver in the form in which they were sent, are accepted. But if the signal pattern is disturbed by someone moving in the protected area, the receiver receives the signal in an altered form and immediately activates the alarm. But false alarms are easily caused by draughts, general movement of the air, sound waves (telephone bell).

With an alarm delay device, the alarm does not sound for a few seconds after the system has been triggered by the intruder so as not to disclose to him which of his actions triggered it. This may confuse him and if he or his friends want to make a return visit, he will not be any wiser what to avoid to counteract the system.

signalling

An alarm system depends for its effectiveness on somebody taking immediate action (even if the action is only the burglar running away). The signalling or alerting is achieved in different ways:

alarm bell or siren is housed in a metal or plastic box installed on the outside of your house as high as possible. When the alarm is activated, the bell rings or siren sounds and continues to do so until someone comes to check the premises and switch the alarm off. (Having one of these boxes on the outside of your house may help to put off an intending burglar who sees it. On the other hand, it might alert the burglar to valuables within and to the need to neutralise the alarm system.)

automatic 999 dialler is a small machine linked to an ordinary telephone line. It should be a separate line for outgoing calls only. When the alarm is activated, the machine automatically dials the local emergency number (usually 999) and a continuous tape calls for police and gives the address of the premises, says that it is an automatic burglar alarm and that the premises have been entered. With some diallers, an alarm bell will also go off either immediately or after some predetermined delay.

direct line termination transmits the signals from your alarm by private line to the alarm company's central station. The line is constantly monitored electronically by the alarm company and if an alarm signal is received, the staff immediately call the police – or anyone else you have nominated to be called. In some areas, the termination point is not the alarm company, but the local police station.

digital communicator is a small machine linked to the ordinary telephone line. When activated, it dials the alarm company central station and sends a coded signal to an automatic receiver which records details of the alarm and informs the alarm company staff who then react in a previously agreed way.

Whatever type of alarm signalling you have, someone must hold the keys of your house, so that if the alarm is activated and the police arrive, there is someone who can let them in to check the house. The police do not hold keys but, when notified of the installation, must be given details of the persons who hold keys. The police may stipulate that there be two or three keyholders, that they should be on the telephone, live reasonably near and/or have their own transport. In some areas, the police have first of all to approve the installation; and they may stipulate that after the alarm has gone off, the resetting of the 999 signalling be done by the alarm company.

the disadvantages
Alarm systems have a nasty tendency to go into an alarm state when the premises are, in fact, secure. You may have failed to set it correctly; equipment may be faulty; telephone engineers working on the line; contacts accidentally activated by the wind rattling and shaking windows and doors that do not fit well; pets, children or insomniacs wandering about.

The different types of signalling also have their disadvantages.

A bell or a siren annoys the neighbours and unless you have a definite arrangement with a well-disposed neighbour to dial 999, it will probably be ignored anyway. The Control of Pollution Act 1974 includes the offence of committing a nuisance by noise (such as an intruder alarm might cause). An automatic cut-out device can be fitted, which switches the bell or siren off after a predetermined time, say, 20 minutes. However, with most systems, the alarm is then out of action until it has been reset, so that there may be an unprotected interval.

Automatic 999 diallers may misroute on the telephone lines and the call never reach the police. Also, if the line is not 'outgoing only', it can be blocked by an intending intruder dialling the number before he breaks in and leaving his receiver off to let it go on ringing, in order to block the automatic dialling.

Direct terminations using a direct exclusive line, such as to a central station, are silent and are continually monitored, so that if something happens to the line, the alarm company is warned – but they are extremely expensive.

A digital communicator is more efficient than a 999 dialling machine and much cheaper than a private line to the central station.

Any signalling that terminates at the police station and has frequent false alarms will make you unpopular and the police may send you a cross letter – and ultimately will refuse to respond.

choosing an alarm system
Before you decide to buy or rent, and maintain, an alarm system, be aware of the cost which can be high, and the potential nuisance to your own family and neighbours.

If you decide that you do want an alarm, or your insurers make it a condition that you have one, you must make up your mind whether you want it to
- *warn the police so that they can arrest the burglar*
  to do this you need a silent alarm termination

- *make a great deal of noise and scare off the burglar*
  if so, you need bell or siren

- *have two bites at the burglar*
  for this, have a silent alarm which warns the police and which after a predetermined time (say, seven minutes) activates an external bell or siren to scare off the burglars if for any reason the police have not arrived.

In making up your mind about the type and degree of alarm protection you need, get the advice of a police crime prevention officer. If your insurers have stipulated that you should have an alarm system, the insurance surveyor will probably tell you what to install and which alarm company to use (in some cases, insurance companies get commission).

There is a British Standard (BS 4737), which lays down minimum requirements for the installation and maintenance of both audible and remote-signalling systems. Different sections of the BS lay down the requirements for some devices.

The National Supervisory Council for Intruder Alarms (NSCIA) is an inspectorate set up to supervise the implementation of the British Standard. It maintains a register of companies that it has approved as alarm system installers. To be on the register, the company has also to give assurances about the integrity of its employees. A free list of approved installers is available from NSCIA, St Ives House, St Ives Road, Maidenhead, Berkshire SL6 1RD. An NSCIA installer will issue you with a certificate that your installation meets BS 4737 (this may be required by your insurers).

The NSCIA does not inspect every system installed but carries out random inspections. If you have trouble with a system installed by an approved installer (such as, for instance, frequent false alarms), an NSCIA inspector will come to examine it.

There are other companies, too, which install to BS 4737; your insurance company or your local police crime prevention officer may be able to give you the names of reliable local installers. In the Yellow Pages directory, installers are listed under 'Burglar alarms and security systems'.

It would be sensible to get quotations for different types and makes of systems and devices. Someone from the alarm company will have to come and inspect your premises before being able to give such an estimate. Beware of letting anyone from an unknown company into your home – ask for references (and follow them up) and check with the local police whether anything is known against the company. A burglar alarm system to a normal house could cost £350 from one installer and be quoted at £800 by another. Do not accept the first quotation; consult the crime prevention officer to make sure you are not being overcharged.

Most burglar alarm companies operate an obligatory maintenance contract for the initial years, which may include an emergency repair service as well as routine servicing visits. The BS lays down that installations be inspected three or four times a year at regular intervals. (This could cost you around £75 a year.)

It is possible to buy do-it-yourself alarm kits, from locksmiths, d-i-y shops, mail order firms. But the National Supervisory Council for Intruder Alarms does not monitor them. Your insurers may not be too impressed by them – but perhaps your burglar will be.

You are almost certain to have to pay more for a professional installation than if you install a kit yourself or put together your own system. The report in *Handyman Which?* in February 1981 on burglar alarms said that the chief advantages of a d-i-y installation are that you have some degree of being able to design the system yourself and that you do not have to have strangers from an alarm company looking around your house and seeing where you keep valuables. Rather than following a standard layout, your own design can be original, and unknown to a professional-type burglar.

A burglar alarm is no substitute for having good security locks and fitments – and using them.

smoke detectors

There are smoke detectors for use in the home, which give warning of the presence of smoke and can raise an alarm before smouldering has become a flame. Two principal types of detector are available – optical (or photoelectric) and ionisation.

The optical type contains a photoelectric cell which responds to changes in light caused by smoke. The ionisation type contains a tiny radioactive source which produces an electric current: smoke particles emitted by a fire alter the current and trigger the alarm. Optical detectors are generally quicker at detecting slow, smouldering fires; ionisation detectors at detecting a sudden blaze. It is also possible to get a combined ionisation and photoelectric detector.

The alarm is usually a loud buzz or wailing sound. An alarm incorporating a light beam is also available.

Most of the devices are independent battery-powered units; systems to be wired to the mains electricity supply are available (but these, of course, will not work if the mains supply has been cut off by the fire). Siting is a critical factor unless you can afford a unit in every room (detectors cost between £10 and about £35 each). Some detectors can be linked to each other so that if one is triggered off (say, downstairs), the others (say, upstairs) will sound, too.

A limitation of smoke detectors is that they are slow to react to a fire on the other side of a closed door, so that a detector fitted in a passageway or corridor may not react to smoke in an adjacent closed room. Since smoke detectors react to cooking fumes, they may give the alarm unnecessarily if sited in, or near, the kitchen.

At least one detector at each level of the building is desirable: for example, in a two-storey dwelling, one in the hall and another at the upstairs landing outside the bedrooms. The best place to fix one is the ceiling, preferably in the middle not near a corner. If wall-mounted, it should be not lower than a foot below the ceiling. Smoke detectors are not very conspicuous, housed in an off-white round or rectangular plastic casing with a grille or vent slits.

Smoke detectors are not a fit-and-forget safeguard; checking and maintenance is important. To check whether the sounder is working, press the test button. Some detectors have a flashing indicator light which blinks when all is well. A further practical test is to blow smoke towards the detector to make it go off.

Detectors rely on air being able to pass freely through the grille or vents to activate the alarm, so regular vacuum cleaning will prevent the build-up of dust. If cobwebs or any other accumulation of dirt can be seen on the detector, it should be cleaned.

Batteries should be replaced at least once a year as a matter of precautionary routine, unless the manufacturers recommend a shorter interval.

Detectors are constructed to sound an intermittent warning bleep or flash a light when the battery is getting low. As a precautionary routine, batteries should be replaced at least once a year, unless the manufacturer recommends a shorter interval.

The *Handyman Which?* report on smoke detectors in August 1981 gives comparative brand information and results of sensitivity tests.

The report concludes "detectors do not prevent fires. Even if you install smoke detectors, you must not be complacent about fire – detectors warn you only after the fire has started, and only if you are at home to hear the alarm."

Insuring and safeguarding

Insurance does not protect your property nor does it deter a burglar even though you are encouraged by insurers' publicity to imagine that you are buying protection and security.

But if you do have insurance, make sure it is adequate. The sum for which to insure the contents of a home is the total value of the individual articles in it.

To arrive at the sum to be insured, make a list of the contents of each room under such headings as: furniture and carpets; curtains and linen; kitchen equipment and glass, china and cutlery; pictures and ornaments; books; clothes and jewellery; radio and television sets and such equipment as tape and video recorders, hi-fi equipment, musical instruments, typewriters; garden furniture and tools; fuel; food and drink. Mark against each item its current shop price, deducting something for wear and tear. If you think that any article you possess is particularly valuable – for instance, a painting or an antique – have it professionally valued.

If you itemise your possessions in this way, it makes it easier not only to decide the total sum to be insured initially, but also to assess values when renewing your policy or making a claim.

Be careful to adjust your insurance annually to cater for inflation, and review your sum insured when you add to your possessions.

An averaging clause in an insurance policy means that if it turns out that you were under-insured, the amount you get when you make a claim will be reduced proportionately to the under-insurance.

With household contents insurance that is a traditional 'indemnity' policy, if you need to claim, what you get is based on the lost item's value at the time of the loss. With a 'replacement-as-new' policy, the insurance is based on the current cost of a similar article new.

Both types of policies can be index-linked (some insurers insist on this for replacement-as-new policies). This means the sum insured is adjusted in step with the general index of retail prices throughout the year, and you pay the increased premium at the end of the year. If your policy is not index-linked, it is up to you to increase the sum insured as and when necessary.

Most policies have a clause by which payment for any one 'valuable' item is limited to a percentage, say 5 per cent or 10 per cent, of the total sum insured, or to not more than, say, £500 or £1000. There is also usually a limit on what will be paid for lost cash, currency notes, bank notes or stamps (check how much this is, it may be as little as £50).

Tell your insurers if you have any individual valuables which are worth more than the unspecified 'valuables' limits; they should be specified in the policy schedule, otherwise the insurers will not pay more than the limit stated. Similarly, if the total value of all 'valuables' comes to more than, say, one third of the total sum insured or £xxx, the amount paid in all for such 'valuables' will be restricted to the limit. But you may increase the normal policy limits on 'valuables' by paying a higher premium.

It is wise to have replacement-as-new cover if you are buying on credit or for items on hire purchase, and to specify the value of any such articles if it is more than the policy's single item limit.

Insurance for a rented TV set can be taken out comparatively cheaply through the rental company.

When you acquire any valuable items which should be specifically included on your policy, inform the insurers straightaway rather than waiting until you renew your policy, so that the items are covered straightaway.

'all-risks'
Although not relevant to burglary, the extra cover given by what is called 'all-risks' insurance is for accidental damage of unexplained loss, including when an item is out of the house. All-risks insurance can be either a separate policy or an all-risks section in a contents policy. You

have to specify the full value of each individual item as the sum insured.

It is also possible to have all-risks cover for unspecified articles of value (jewellery, generally) and possibly for clothing. There is usually a maximum limit for any one article as well as a total limit under this particular section.

All-risks insurance is not index-linked, even if it is part of a contents policy that is index-linked, so you should check your sums insured regularly.

keeping a record
Valuations and receipts for things you have acquired should be kept somewhere safe (and not with the items themselves), against the time that your insurers might want proof of value.

For jewellery, a regular updating of its value for insurance purposes by a reputable jeweller is advisable. Other experts or professional valuers would need to be consulted for pictures, precious items, collections, porcelain and other valuable objects. Find out on what basis the valuer will charge you – generally, the fee is a percentage of the amount he values your possessions at.

Having a professional valuation, although expensive, will eliminate many queries and speed up the claims process when trying to assess the value of any articles that get stolen.

There is no need to give the valuer or jeweller your address; all sorts of people may have access to his records and someone might use them as the basis of a burglar's 'shopping list'.

It may be a counsel of perfection, but it can be useful to record property acquired over the years by keeping receipts or entering a note of what was bought, when, where and for how much, in an exercise book or file. Gifts, too, can be recorded in this way. An entry in your book at the time will enable you to make a realistic assessment of the value in the future.

One insurance company has this advice printed on its policy: 'Do not wait until you have a claim to make sure you understand your policy – please read it now and keep it in a safe place. In particular, make sure that all the details shown in the policy schedule are correct (let us know immediately if any change is necessary).'

identification
It is important to be able to give accurate descriptions to the police when property is stolen and to be able to identify your property positively if it is recovered after being stolen. With items such as TV sets, hi-fi equipment, kitchen and household appliances that are mass-produced, yours looks like anyone else's and if it is stolen and then recovered, you may have some difficulty in identifying it conclusively as yours.

All electrical equipment has a small plate somewhere on it which, among other information, gives a serial number peculiar to that one item. Make a note of the make, type and serial numbers of all your electrical equipment, down to your daughter's hair dryer, and keep the record in a safe place.

Identification plates, however, can be removed, and sometimes they are. It is possible to buy an inexpensive security marking pen that marks invisibly. With one of these, you can mark your own property by writing your name and address on it or, shorter, just your postcode, with the number of your house added at the end (or name, if it has no number). Because the mark fades into invisibility quickly, make a note of where you are putting it, in case you should need to tell the police at some later stage (or alter it when you move house). It is visible only when subjected to ultra violet light. The police have equipment to make the mark visible and from the postcode will be able to tell where the article came from.

Alternatively, you can engrave your identifying mark on furniture, tape recorder, TV set, typewriter.

Jewellery, silver and glassware, porcelain, some pictures, objets d'art can be very difficult to describe so as to be recognisable from your description. There are firms specialising in photographing valuable objects for identification purposes, should they be stolen. The firm takes the photographs on their premises or in your home. You, the owner, get the prints and negatives, or the firm may offer to store the prints and negatives for you under secure conditions, to be produced if and when required. Make sure it is a reputable firm, otherwise you could be providing an illustrated catalogue for burglars.

But it is probably wiser to do your own photography. If your own camera is not adequate for the job or you yourself are not competent, get an experienced amateur photographer friend to do it. Each item must stand clear of any other item; you may need to have more than one view of some items. Make sure that if the object to be photographed has any identifying features, such as damage or distinctive marks, they are clearly visible and defined. Photograph small items with a 12-inch ruler or a matchbox or coin next to them, to give an indication of their true size. Number the prints and keep the negatives in a safe place.

If you are keeping an inventory book of your property, write down where and when you bought an object, how much it cost, any serial numbers and any identifying features; also where on the object you have put the 'invisible' postcode. Also note down in the book any important numbers such as that of your national savings book, building society pass book, credit cards (so that if you should need to report their loss, you can quote the number), and the number of your insurance policy.

Of course, this inventory book should be kept somewhere where it is unlikely to be found by anyone else, and not with any of the valuable items.

safekeeping

Do not keep your spare money, jewellery or valuables which mean much to you in a conventional place such as in a jewellery box on the dressing table or a desk drawer, even if locked. Divide it up and keep it in plastic bags or some inconspicuous-looking box and hide them in different non-conventional places, the more original and less readily accessible, the better (some of the money may be in a book on the top shelf). Then it does not matter so much if the burglar finds the jewellery box or breaks into the desk.

If you have valuables such as silver, coins or similar collections, or jewellery not regularly in use, consider depositing some or all in your bank or a security vault.

If you want to deposit valuables or documents with your bank, you should ask the branch manager what facilities he can offer. Generally, you can leave a locked box or other sealed container in the bank's strongroom for an annual or half-yearly fee, depending on the size of the container (say, 50p for an envelope for 6 months or £5 for a small box). Insurance of the contents is your responsibility; the bank does not need – or want – to know what is inside; you keep the key of your own box and can have access to the box or container (occasionally there may be a charge for this) or withdraw it at any time. The procedure varies from bank to bank and involves identification, signature card and other documents.

For short term deposits, such as for holiday periods, there may be a minimum charge at the 6 months' rate – or no charge at all, if your bank manager is well disposed towards you.

In a few city branches of the main banks, there may be space in a safe deposit section where you can rent your own locked drawer or small safe, for which the bank will also hold a key. But there is usually a waiting list for a place in a security vault, and the rental is fairly high.

Tell your insurers when you have put anything into safekeeping: the saving on the reduced insurance premium is likely to more than offset the deposit fee charged. If you want to take an item out of deposit for any period, you should tell the insurers and ask for it to be covered while you have it out – you may have to pay an extra premium for this time.

safes

Whatever you may have done to improve the security of your home and however good you may now feel that it is, you may still be reluctant to have smaller valuable property, jewellery, important documents, passports and so on, just lying around the house and may start thinking in terms of a home safe.

Safes are available from specialist security firms who do the installing; also from locksmiths and by mail order for installation by a handyman or the local builder.

Which safe you choose to have installed will be dictated by
- the type and value of the property to be kept in it
- the physical bulk of that property
- the requirements of your insurers (who may specify the type and the model).

There are three types of safe: wall safes, underfloor safes and free-standing safes.

Handyman Which? February 1981 included a report on some low-priced wall safes and an underfloor safe.

The type of safe you install may determine the amount of cover your insurers will allow – but other security factors in your home affect this, too. Before spending (a lot of) money on a safe, check that your insurers will recognise it to the extent of fully insuring the contents.

wall safes
Sizes of wall safes are traditionally given in 'bricks', in terms of the number of standard house bricks that would need to be removed to fit the safe into the wall. The smallest is the size of one brick, a large one is five bricks high and requires a wall or chimney breast at least 14 in thick in which to install it. Most manufacturers make only one or two sizes, and quote the outside and inside dimensions.

As their name implies, wall safes are fitted into a wall, so the first requirement is for a substantially built wall of sufficient thickness to accept the safe. These safes are usually either screwed or rawlbolted into the wall, or are cemented-in. Unless a wall safe is very securely installed, it can be fairly easily prised out of the wall and removed bodily. Wall safes tend to be hidden behind a curtain, picture, or in the side or rear of a fitted cupboard, but these are the standard places so, if you can, have yours put into a more original, not too obvious place.

underfloor safes
Underfloor safes are usually square-bodied, or cylindrical-shaped. They are available in several sizes – the most popular about 12 in by 12 in by 12 in. On top of the body of the safe there is a neck or throat, usually circular, about 6 in diameter and about 6 in deep into which fits the safe door. This means that the bottom of an underfloor safe is going to be about 18 in below the floor level.

The safe can be anywhere on the ground floor provided the floor itself is suitable (and that there are no pipes, cables or water course concealed under the floor at the chosen position). It is the concreting-in that provides security, so you would not install an underfloor safe into an upstairs wooden floor.

After installation, the hole is covered by a form of trapdoor and concealed with the carpet or a rug. The size of the door (usually about 6 in diameter) is a drawback because it restricts what you can put in the safe. Also, you have to get down on to your hands and knees to get at it.

freestanding safes
A freestanding safe is what is usually thought of when the word 'safe' is mentioned – solid, squarish, usually standing in full view unless concealed by a cupboard built around it.

Freestanding safes are usually available in four or five sizes, ranging from about 20 in by 18 in by 18 in and weighing about 5 cwt, to 72 in by 36 in by 30 in and weighing about $2\frac{1}{2}$ tons; there are larger ones for commercial premises. The door is almost as large as the front elevation of the safe, which makes it fairly easy to put in bulky articles.

Get the supplier, or surveyor or a builder, to advise you whether your floor is strong enough to support the size of safe you intend to have, otherwise it might crash straight through the floor.

A freestanding safe, particularly one that weighs under 20 cwt, should be rawlbolted to the floor or wall or, in the case of a wooden floor, anchored with 'U' bolts that pass under the joists and are secured inside the safe, to prevent bodily removal of the safe.

locks
Most freestanding safes are supplied with either a keylock (with a minimum of 7 levers) or a keyless combination lock. A safe may have two locks, one of each type, or both of either.

For wall safes and underfloor safes, keylocks are standard, but some can be supplied with a keyless combination lock if required.

Keyless combination locks are slightly more expensive but there is no key to lose, no keyhole for a thief to try to pick the lock through or in which to place explosives in an attempt to blow the lock off. You can change the combination at any time if you should want to, or feel it necessary.

keeping it safe
If you have a lot to hide securely, it may be worth having a second safe (put in by a different installer) located in an even less conventional place, even if less convenient. Spread the load: in case of burglary, there is a chance that you will lose the contents of only one of the safes.

Do not tell anybody about it who does not need to know that you have a safe, let alone where it is. Better not to tell even the children, in case they tell others.

The car gets left in the open, on the street, in all sorts of places, frequently unlocked and with the keys left in the ignition because "I'll only be two minutes".

It is an open invitation for
– the car itself to be stolen
– accessories such as the radio or cassette player to be stolen from it
– loose property left in the car to be stolen.

Securing your car against any of these is neither difficult nor particularly expensive.

Protecting property left in the car is more a matter of discipline and thought than anything else. Always wind up the windows (shut and latch quarter lights) and lock all the doors of the car when you leave it.

When leaving property in the car, put it in the boot and lock it. The boot lock is not particularly secure but if property cannot be seen, it does not provide a temptation. Speculative breaking-in to car boots is not a common practice.

For the occasions when you have to leave a briefcase or a suitcase or shopping bags in the car, even for a short while, carry a small rug or mat or blanket or similar cover. Leave your belongings in the back of the car, not on the front seat, and put the neutral-looking cover over them. Those stealing from cars prefer to see what they hope to steal before deciding to break into a car.

Try to fit accessories where they are not obvious – for example, stereo speakers not sitting on the back shelf where they call attention to the fact that you have a stereo unit fitted. A cassette player fitted out of sight under the dashboard is just as easy to use and is much more likely to remain there than if it is fitted in a position where it is immediately visible to a casual passer-by. The cassettes themselves are better stored in a small case out of sight – under the seat, for instance. Make a note of the serial number of the car radio or cassette player by which it could be identified if stolen and recovered.

If your car is one of the more popular marques and types and you have fitted special 'go fast' alloy wheels, fit security wheel nuts, one to each wheel, otherwise those wheels may not still be there when you return to the car. There are two kinds, one incorporating a cylinder keylock and the other requiring a special spanner with pegs corresponding to holes in the security nut.

locking

Car door locks generally do not have any great security value, but you can get special locks fitted to the doors, boot and bonnet. For instance, mortise rack bolts that are operated only from the inside of the car and invisible from the outside can be fitted to the rear and front passenger doors, and to the driver's door a key-operated rack bolt that is operated from the outside. (Mortise rack bolts also can be fitted to the side edges of a hatchback door.) Since these bolts are additional to the locks fitted as standard, a would-be thief has two locks to overcome. An alternative would be to change the locks on the front doors for deadlocking cylinders, but this may be a hazard in a crash because a door that is deadlocked cannot be opened from the outside without a key.

It is possible to get duplicate ignition keys cut for some cars, provided you know the key number. Some criminals specialising in thefts of and from cars carry miniature telescopes to enable them to read the cylinder number of ignition locks through the window from outside the car. Most new cars nowadays do not show the number, but if yours does, cover it with a small piece of sticky paper or tape, or a tiny dab of paint. (Make sure that you have made a note of the number somewhere else, before you obliterate it on the car.)

immobilising

One way of ensuring that your car is still where you left it when you return, is to resort to the old wartime method of immobilisation: remove the rotor arm. But this can cause damage if done too often or clumsily.

There are other ways of achieving immobilisation. One is by an electrical cut-out, which amounts to wiring a concealed switch into the ignition system. The car cannot then be started until the switch is found and has been thrown. Another device scrambles the firing order of the plugs – the engine will not start until the device has been unscrambled. There are other methods of preventing the car from starting, such as cutting off the fuel supply or the battery.

All models of cars produced since 1970 are fitted with an anti-theft device as standard, so the majority of cars on the road today probably have a gear change lock or a transmission lock, or most commonly a steering lock. A back-up to a steering lock is to fit a device which locks the clutch to the steering wheel by means of an extendable lockable bar hooked on to each. This inhibits any movement of either, therefore preventing the gears from being engaged or the car from being steered. (A chain and padlock can be used in a similar way.) This device, because it is easily visible from the outside, is usually effective in deterring the youngster who is trying to 'borrow' your car, to go for a joy ride.

But none of this can stop an organised set of crooks coming along with a recovery vehicle, winching your car up and taking it away to a place where they can work on it in peace.

alarms
Car alarms are designed to give warning that the car is being taken or tampered with and, with luck, to scare off the thief. There are various forms of alarms, such as electric contacts on doors, boot or bonnet so that any attempt to enter the car or steal from the boot or interfere with the engine sets off the alarm.

Tremblers can be set in the boot or under the bonnet; they are activated if the car is rocked or subjected to vibrations. These have the disadvantage that the local kids soon discover this and delight in giving the car a quick shake as they pass, to set the alarm off.

A rather more expensive type of alarm uses inertia switches which require a build-up of vibration: a single knock will not set them off, but a series of vibrations caused, for instance, by someone fiddling with the locks, will do so. There are a number of variations on these basic themes, and some combinations of immobiliser and alarm.

The alarm signalling varies, some using the car horn, others using a special horn or siren, some causing the headlamps to flash on and off as well. Most use the car battery for power and may run it down if no one comes to switch off the signal and there is no automatic cut-out. A few are self-powered from separate dry batteries; they emit a weaker signal and the storage life of such batteries is limited.

The majority of car security systems are available as d-i-y kits which are reasonably easy for the competent handyperson to install.

A window sticker that tells a prospective thief that your car has an anti-theft device fitted may deter him from even attempting to steal the car. But do not use window stickers that say which particular device you have fitted – the thief may have done his homework and know how to deal with it.

identification
In case your car should get stolen, there are ways of marking it to make identification easier if the police recover the car. A name, number or mark could be indelibly inscribed on a window or engraved on metalwork.

If your car is stolen by a professional and then resprayed and fitted with new number plates, chassis number and so on, it can be quite difficult to prove that the car really is (or was) yours. Therefore, put some identification marks on the car where only you know about them – in the boot, under a carpet, inside a door trim, for instance. The 'invisible' marking pen can also be used on an inside part of the car.

Never carry your car documents in the car.

when your car is stolen

When you return and cannot find the car, first think whether it may have been towed away by the police for illegal parking. In a crowded side street or a big car park, it is as well to make quite sure you remember where you leave the car. The police are inclined to cross-examine you closely as to where you left it and they take a dim view if, after all, the car is not stolen but you have simply forgotten where it is.

If the car has really gone, inform the police straightaway – either the first passing policeman or by ringing the local police station. It is not a '999' situation unless you had left the car for just a few minutes – or come back to see it actually being driven away.

Then go to the nearest police station or to the one you have been told to report to, confirm that your car has been stolen, and give as full details as possible. If the car has not been recovered within a couple of days, you will have to give the police investigating officer all the details from the registration document, such as chassis number, engine number, cubic capacity, year of manufacture.

If the car has got some mark or something by which you can subsequently identify it if it is eventually recovered, describe this to the police.

claiming on insurance

Provided you have comprehensive motor insurance, or a third party, fire and theft policy, a claim can be made on your insurance policy if the car itself is stolen, or parts of it. A comprehensive policy also covers loss of luggage or personal effects from the car. Your first action after reporting to the police that your car has been stolen, is to notify your insurers.

Many cars are only 'borrowed' either for joy-riding or for criminal purposes, and abandoned afterwards. Insurers therefore usually wait for, say, six weeks or so before meeting a claim for a stolen car, to see whether the car is recovered. For this reason, some companies do not ask you to fill in a claim form straightaway. A few policies include the cost of hiring a car for a limited period (usually two weeks) while yours is out of action: that would include when stolen.

If the car is not recovered, an offer is made to you by the insurers usually on a total loss basis – that is, you get its secondhand value at the time it is stolen. (Some insurers offer "new car concession" cover whereby if the car is less than 12 months old, they are willing to replace it with a brand new car.) Should the car subsequently be recovered when the claim has been settled, it becomes the property of the insurers.

Even if your car is recovered in a matter of hours, you should report its temporary loss to the insurers (as well as to the police). You may need to claim subsequently on your policy as a result of some damage, not obvious when the car is first recovered, that was done while it was out of your possession. Also, things in the car may have been stolen from it, for which you may be able to claim. Moreover, the car may have been involved in an accident while it was being driven by the thief, and may even have killed somebody. A witness may have noted the car and its number but not noticed the driver, and if you have not reported the loss of your vehicle promptly, the suspicion may fall on you. While your car is driven by someone without your permission, it is uninsured for damage done by it and your insurers will not pay.

There is a limit (usually £50) to the amount paid by insurers on claims for articles stolen out of the car, such as a rug or camera. If only your car radio or cassette player is taken, these count as personal effects even though fitted in the car, and the limit applies. The cassettes themselves also count as personal effects.

The 'temporarily removed' section of a contents policy may cover loss of personal articles that you carry with you in your car. If you have all-risks insurance, either separately or as part of a household contents policy, claim on that for any valuables taken with or from the car.

Claiming on the car policy may cost you your no-claims discount. Ask your insurers before you formally claim whether doing so would jeopardise your no-claims discount, so that you can calculate whether it is worth it.

When you are burgled

So, the worst has happened, you come home and find the place all upside down: you have been burgled. What do you do? The first thing is not to lose your head and rush around trying to put everything straight. Do not touch anything. Telephone the police.

The quicker you let the police know, the sooner they can act: the burglar may still be nearby. (If your telephone is out of action, use a neighbour's.) To call the police, dial the local emergency number or 999 and ask for the police, who will then send an officer to deal with the situation.

Heed any instructions or guidance the police give you on the telephone, and make a note of which police station you were put through to.

With a bit of luck, your burglar will have left some fingerprints somewhere and, with a bit more luck, the police may find them – but not if you have touched things and obliterated any prints there may be. Using gloves or a handkerchief to open doors is, if anything, counter-productive. A fingerprint is basically the deposit of body sweat. Touching articles with a cloth, or similar, will wipe away all trace. It is better that the police should find an over-print, or partial print from your hand, than nothing at all. You and the family should be prepared to have your own fingerprints taken, so that your prints can be eliminated. (The copies of your fingerprints will later be destroyed by the police.) There are bound to be scores of fingerprints all over the place, belonging to you and your household, but there is always the chance that your intruder may have left the odd one, and that is the one the police do not want you to obliterate. To reveal any prints there may be, a special powder is put over all the likely areas.

While waiting for the police, go from room to room to get a quick impression of what has been taken and how much damage has been done. Use your eyes not your hands – do not touch anything at all.

The uniformed police constable who comes will take the necessary particulars to initiate action. A plain clothes CID (criminal investigation department) officer may then come to continue the investigations. A police constable is the same rank and status as a detective constable albeit that one wears a uniform and the other does not. CID officers attend most but not all burglaries; even if an officer in civilian clothes does not appear at your house, the investigation behind the scenes is supervised by a senior detective. Another non-uniformed person who might come is the scene-of-crimes officer, a civilian specialist attached to the police force who looks for fingerprints and takes samples for likely clues.

All bureaucratic organisations go about things according to their established rule and practice. The police force's bureaucratic methods prove to be generally effective, even when their style and manner appear low-keyed. Do not get too impatient when they seem to you not to be attaching the importance to your burglary that you do, and remember that they are probably dealing with a dozen similar break-ins at the same time.

Be prepared to give the CID as many facts as possible about what you have noticed (for instance, doors opened that are usually shut, unusual footprints in the garden, strangers having recently called at your home – anything at all which may yield useful clues) as well as details of your own and your family's movements. Neighbours can be asked whether they have seen anything or anyone strange.

If you can, write it all down. When the police arrive (or you call at the police station), give your written story to them. They may learn more from reading it than merely from your answers to their questions, and they may have a better idea what to ask more about.

Make a note of the name or number of the officer dealing with your case and where he can be contacted, so that you can get in touch with him easily if necessary at a later stage.

Always notify the police of any incidents of illicit entry to your home and of any burglary, even when you think that the incident was small, that you lost little or nothing, that notifying the police will not help you and may mean extra bother. Regard it at least as your social good deed towards communal security. By telling the police, you give them the knowledge of what is happening in the area so that they will have a better picture of all the incidents and will be better able to find the right means to prevent the same thing happening to you and your neighbours in the future.

what has gone

The police (and your insurers) will want a list of property that is missing. Some things you will notice right away, others you may not discover until you start tidying up and putting things straight after the police have told you that you may do so.

Make an examination of each room in order to prepare a list of articles that are missing. It is important that details of items that can be positively identified are given to the police at the earliest possible opportunity. These can then be circulated to the police forces in whose area the goods may appear, so that they can be quickly related to the break-in at your home. The incised or 'invisible' postcode with house number suffix will help trace the article back to you. This is the stage where you should tell the police where you hid the invisible mark. It is also the stage when those lists of serial numbers and those photographs that you took, prove invaluable. If you can say that the kitchen food mixer was an ABC make, serial number 132457, and "Here is a photograph of the pair of George III candlesticks that have gone", the police know exactly what they are looking for. With luck, they may even know the 'fence' likely to have them.

When you give a list of missing items to the police, say that it is only complete as far as you know at the time. If you later realise that other belongings have gone, inform the police at once.

lost credit cards and keys
One of the first things to check is whether the burglar has taken any credit card or cheque book or travellers cheques. Until the issuing organisation and bank are notified, you may have to carry the loss if money or credit is obtained on your account. A lost credit card can – and should – be reported at any hour of the day or night. If you have not made a note of the telephone number to ring, you can get it from the statements or another cardholder's card.

Another urgent matter is to see if any identified keys have been taken, such as one labelled "spare front door" or "garage" or "No 15's". In all these cases, it would be advisable to get the locks or at least the cylinder or lever mechanism changed.

If you have been burgled by a professional, you should review your security: the burglar may have seen things which were of no interest to him but which might interest a friend of his. For example, a jewel thief may take jewellery only, leaving fur coat, silver, TV set which are valuable but not of interest to him. But it means that a second burglary is quite likely, so the security arrangements and locks should be changed.

If you hold keys to someone else's house and that house is burgled, stand by for trouble – yours may be the first house searched by the police looking for the missing property. Even if they are satisfied, the other person's insurers will be interested in you and whether any element of negligence on your part may have contributed to the loss.

insurance claim

Tell your insurers as soon as possible that you have had a break-in and that you want to make a claim on your policy. It is helpful to indicate the potential loss involved, but you do not have to send off a list of stolen property to them until you can be fairly sure that you have included everything.

All insurance policies contain conditions dealing specifically with claims. Look out your policy to see what you should do. Some policies call for notification of an impending claim to be made in writing, others suggest a telephone call as the initial notification. Some insurers now issue a claim advice form with every new policy, which can be used to notify any claim without delay.

The usual requirements of insurers following a burglary are that you
- notify the police immediately
- tell the insurers of the loss as soon as reasonably possible
- provide the insurers with full details of the property stolen.

If it is essential to carry out emergency repairs to make the property secure again and reduce the possibility of a second break-in, check that the cost of these emergency repairs is covered under your policy (buildings or contents). Keep the bills or receipts for the work.

through a broker
If you used a broker to take out the policy for you with an insurance company, you can ask him to help negotiate a claim on the policy. He is not obliged to do this – brokers are paid by insurers for bringing business, not claims – but it would be unusual for a broker not to help you. You should ask him whether he will charge you for handling the claim.

With an insurance policy at Lloyd's, you will have to claim through a Lloyd's broker. You do not deal with a Lloyd's syndicate direct; all correspondence is handled by the broker and all claims must be notified to him and he passes them on to the underwriters and deals with them. A Lloyd's broker does not charge for handling a claim on a Lloyd's policy.

loss assessors
There are individuals and firms who operate as 'loss assessors', giving advice on the preparation, negotiation and settlement of insurance claims on behalf of the insured person. Because of his past experience with claims and his knowledge of policies and conditions and market values, a loss assessor may be able to recover more from insurers than a claimant would on his own.

A loss assessor will charge you a fee for handling your claim. The fee is negotiable, and you should ask beforehand what it is likely to be and what it will cover. Fees are related to the amount you get in settlement from your insurers: for instance, 10 per cent if the amount recovered is less than £1000. The percentage should go down as the amount of the claim goes up so that for a claim resulting in a payment of, say, £50,000, the assessor's fee might be in the region of £1500, depending on the particular assessor and the type of claim involved.

If anyone turns up on your doorstep or rings up after you have had an extensive burglary and offers to handle your insurance claim for you, check his credentials carefully. For example, you should ask for the names of individuals or firms whom he has acted for, so that you can ask them for their comments on the standard and value of his services.

There is an Institute of Public Loss Assessors whose members have to comply with a code of conduct, professional ethics and practice. To get a list of members of the IPLA, send a stamped self-addressed envelope to the honorary general secretary at 14 Red Lion Street, Chesham, Bucks HP5 1HB.

claim form
You can claim on a contents policy for any article stolen, or damaged

as a result of the burglary. You would have to claim on your buildings policy (or, if you are a tenant, generally your landlord on his) for damage done to part of the house – such as windows broken, doors bashed in, locks damaged, garden fence or gate knocked down.

You will be sent a claim form to complete. Insurers generally use the same claim form for different claims, to cut down on the number of different forms in use. The form will probably have been designed to cater for various types of claim and some of the questions on the form you get may have no relevance to the claim you are making. Merely write "Not applicable" (or n/a) against any such questions. Never leave the answer to a question blank: this is nearly always queried. If you do not know the answer to a question or cannot understand what information is being sought, say so, either by writing a note on the form or in a covering letter when returning it.

You will have to give factual details of the burglary, the date and time, who discovered it, at which police station it has been reported. The insurers will wish to know whether any other insurance is in force covering any of the property stolen and whether any other party has an interest in any of the articles stolen, such as hire purchase or TV rental company.

Anything which you are buying on hire purchase or paying for by instalments through a credit arrangement can be claimed for; you will get its current market value or replacement cost but not the extra cost of buying on credit. You will have to go on making your instalment payments for it even though it is no longer in your possession – unless you pay off the outstanding debt now with a lump sum payment.

If you were renting the TV set, tell the rental company immediately that it has been stolen: you will be liable to pay the rent until then. If your insurance for the set was through the rental company, they will claim on the insurance on your behalf.

If the set was insured under your household contents policy, tell the insurers that the set was a rented one, and given them the name and address of the rental company so that they can find out the value of the set at the time of its loss. They may pay the company direct. In most cases, you can start a new rental agreement straightaway, and get another set without waiting for reimbursement for the stolen one.

what you claim for
The part of the claim form which is more difficult to complete is where you have to describe precisely what articles have been stolen and state the amount claimed for each.

The information you have to give for each item covers

- description
  This should be as detailed as possible: a TV set, for example, should be identified by make, screen size, colour or black and white, portable, remote control. Whereas in the description to the police, the aim is to give identifying details in the hope of recovering the item, for insurance the details given should be those that help to establish its value. For example, for "clock", put down, say, "late 18th century carriage clock" or "digital radio-alarm clock".

- date when acquired
  You may have kept the bills or receipts (with dates) for some items, but many pieces may have been old, inherited or received as a gift, and precise dates not known. For these, wherever possible, insert the approximate year or outline the history of acquiring them.

- original purchase price
  Old bills, receipts or chequebook stubs would provide the answer, but in most cases they will have been thrown away. When the answer becomes a test of memory, you can only do your best. For gifts and inherited items, it is even more difficult to be accurate – how can you know what your late grandparents paid for that silver tea service they gave you as a wedding present more than 20 years ago?

Nowadays the question of original cost is not so relevant because replacement cost is the starting point for most insurance claims.

- cost to replace today
  This is no problem for items currently available in the shops. When the identical article is no longer available, insert the current cost of the nearest equivalent to the stolen item.

- value at time of loss
  A deduction will have to be made for wear and tear unless the policy is for replacement-as-new.

- value of salvage
  When insurers pay for a loss, they deduct the value of any part of the property that can be salvaged – but this would not apply where goods are stolen and not recovered.

- amount claimed
  This depends on the type of cover provided by the policy.

With a replacement-as-new policy, you claim the cost of buying a new article for each one that is stolen or totally destroyed. For clothing and household linen, a deduction has to be made to allow for the age or wear and tear of the lost articles. Some policies only pay the replacement cost of articles that are less than a certain number of years old (generally 2 or 3 or 5 years).

With a traditional 'indemnity' policy, you have to assess the state of each article at the time of the burglary and take off an amount to allow for the difference between the cost of replacing it with a new one and the use you had had out of the stolen one. For example, a carpet bought ten years ago for £100 could well cost £500 to replace today and you should have been increasing the sum insured on that basis. As it has had, say, half its serviceable life, the amount the insurers pay would be 50 per cent of today's replacement cost – £250. On the other hand, a cut glass bowl will not have depreciated through age or wear and tear, so the amount to claim is the present cost of a new one.

what you will get
However great your loss, you can never get in all from the insurers more than the total sum insured for which you have been paying the premium.

Most replacement-as-new policies are index-linked. So, as long as you initially insured for the full amount of the then current value and you have added the value of any items subsequently acquired, the sum insured now should be adequate for the cost of replacements.

With an indemnity policy, you will get the 'used' value which takes into account the age and condition of the lost pieces.

for all-risks
If you have an all-risks policy with different insurers from your household contents, both insurers should be notified of the theft as soon as is reasonably practicable.

If any article specified in an all-risks insurance policy is stolen, the maximum amount you can claim is the sum insured, irrespective of today's replacement cost.

Most all-risks insurance is not index-linked, so if you have not revised the sum insured, you may find that it is no longer adequate. If the current value is less – for example, a 15 year old fur coat – you will get no more than its current value (unless the insurance was on an 'agreed value' basis, in which case you will get whatever sum was agreed). On the other hand, if the value of the item has gone up (say, a gold ring), you will get no more than the sum for which you had insured it.

To claim for 'unspecified' articles, you have to list them and will not get for any one item more than the maximum limit stated in the policy. When items are covered as 'unspecifieds' in all-risks insurance as well as 'valuables' in a contents policy, only one policy will pay out. Claim on all-risks where such an item would not be fully covered by the single item limit of a contents policy.

Where money is covered by both policies, you can claim the limit on the contents policy (say, £50 or £100) and the rest up to the limit of the all-risks insurance. But there may be an 'excess' of, say, £15 on the cover for money, which means that you get £15 less than you claim.

Most claim forms ask you to supply receipts or valuations for items specified in an all-risks policy or section, unless these were sent to the insurers when the cover was arranged.

for repairs
On the claim form, put down any damage to the home caused by the intruders: for instance, breaking windows, locks, bolts and doors to gain access. If there has been malicious damage at the same time, such as tomato sauce being thrown all over the walls, a contribution towards redecoration can also be part of your claim.

Before any major work is done, insurers usually wish to see estimates for repairing the damage.

A policy of indemnity, such as a buildings policy, means that the insured person must not be placed in a position better than he was in before the loss. So, the insurers pay only the proportion of the cost that gets you back to the same state as before. For instance, if the window was in a dilapidated state before it was damaged by the burglar, you may have to pay your share for the improvement there will be after the new one has been put in. The amount for 'betterment' may be open to negotiation if you think the deduction the insurers suggest is too high.

the next step
Before you send off the completed claim form, take a photocopy of it (and of the enclosures). The next step depends on the nature and extent of your claim.

Both the police and insurers will be hoping that your property will be traced. But if you hear nothing for, say, two weeks, get in touch with the insurers.

With a small claim, you may get a cheque in settlement without further discussion or delay. In other cases, the insurers may want to have more information and to discuss the claim before settlement. For this purpose, the insurers will arrange for someone to call on you as soon as possible. (A personal visit to your home provides an opportunity to assess the value of what is lost in relation to its setting.) The person who comes may be one of their own officials, an experienced claims handler, or a professional loss adjuster from an independent firm, whose fee is paid by your insurers.

Loss adjusters work exclusively for insurers, including Lloyd's syndicates, and are not employed by individual members of the public. They have their own professional bodies, the Chartered Institute of Loss Adjusters and the Insurance Adjusters Association.

A loss adjuster is appointed to scrutinise a claim and to report to the insurers on it; he will check the amounts or the values you are claiming. Loss adjusters have their fingers on the pulse of general market trends and know how much things are currently worth. The object is to ensure that, within the terms of the policy, you receive no more and no less than fair financial compensation for your loss.

A loss adjuster does not just turn up at your home, but fixes an appointment beforehand. When someone comes, ask for proof, such as a letter of authority, that he is a person appointed by your insurers. If in doubt, telephone the company (or your broker) and check before giving the person any information. Sensible precautions will not be resented by a genuine loss adjuster.

The loss adjuster will discuss with you any grey areas on the claim form, and will point out the wording on the policy where certain items are not covered, or limits apply. He will try to clarify the basis of settlement in your particular case, especially with regard to the adequacy of the sum insured at the time of the loss, and the values of items.

Do not be intimidated (especially if you are still psychologically in a state of shock after the burglary); be scrupulously honest, but stand firm.

After the discussion with you, the loss adjuster sends a report to the insurers with his recommendations.

settlement
The insurers will suggest a figure in settlement of your claim. If you accept, you will be asked to sign a discharge form for settlement of the claim in return for the cheque. The form may say that the payment is "in full and final settlement". But, in case you find later that something else had been stolen, you should retain your right to reopen your claim by adding words such as "settlement . . . in relation to those items known at this time to have been lost".

problems
You may realise for the first time that your policy is subject to 'average' (for instance, all-risks insurance and Lloyd's policies are). This means that if the sum for which you had insured comes to only, say, 60 per cent of the real value, the insurers pay only 60 per cent of any loss even if what you have lost is well within the amount of the sum insured. Where there is no average clause, the insurers may also penalise you by paying only a proportion if, by being under-insured, you are in breach of a declaration made when you took the insurance that you would insure for the full value.

Your claim may be turned down altogether if you had failed to follow a specific warranty such as setting the burglar alarm, or if you had not complied with any general policy conditions. This could arise if, for instance, the house had been left insufficiently furnished for occupancy for any length of time (usually over 30 days) without the insurers having been informed. And if any part of your premises is let, no claim for theft will be met unless there is evidence of forcible entry.

You may find that certain items on your claim form have been excluded. Your policy may not cover the theft of other people's possessions –

your guest's or employee's, for instance – unless you had specifically extended it for such circumstances. Anything bought abroad, such as jewellery, or a camera, watch or radio, may not be covered unless you can produce a customs document stating that you had declared the item when you brought it into this country.

In the event of a difficult dispute that cannot be settled between yourself and your insurers, you can ask the Insurance Ombudsman whether he can deal with it. You must do so within six months of your final failure to agree with the insurers. Explain your complaint in a short letter in which you must quote your policy number and the name of your insurers.

The address is Insurance Ombudsman Bureau, 31 Southampton Row, London WC1B 5HJ.

If you have failed to pay the premium, your policy will have lapsed. The insurers would be justified in dismissing your claim if you had let more than a short time go by without paying the premium. However, in some cases of genuine misunderstanding, insurers may make an ex gratia payment, so suggest this to them and offer to pay the outstanding premium now.

after the claim is settled
Even after you have been paid, you may be able to re-open the claim if you realise later that something else was stolen, provided you reserved the right to do so when you signed the discharge form. You will have to give details of the article to the insurers but will not be expected to fill in another claim form.

In most types of insurance, after a claim has been met, the sum insured is reduced by the amount that has been paid to you. After a substantial claim, you should reassess the remaining sum insured in case it would not be adequate if you had to make another claim before renewal. Remember that the total sum insured affects any special percentage limit on valuables. In order to be covered for an adequate sum insured (including cover for anything bought in replacement), until the policy is due to be renewed, you should offer to pay an additional premium (on a pro rata basis) to reinstate the insurance to the full value. In the case of a claim for a small amount – say, under £200 – reinstatement payment is usually waived by the insurers because the work involved in collecting small additional premiums would be uneconomic. Some policies provide for automatic reinstatement of the sum insured without paying an additional premium following a claim.

Your insurers may make it a condition of continuing your insurance that you install security devices such as additional locks or a burglar alarm system to reduce the possibility of further loss or damage. The insurers may insist on a particular brand or make of security device (perhaps they get a commission from that firm). It may not be the make or type you want to have; maybe you can get something as effective at less expense. Get the advice of the police crime prevention officer about alternatives and if the insurers will not agree to your alternative choice, consider changing your insurers.

recovered property
Sometimes stolen property is recovered after a claim has been paid. The police may contact you, asking you to go to the police station to identify the articles. You should inform the insurers immediately, tell them what has been recovered and say either that you would like to have the articles back or that the insurers can have them and when they can be collected (from your address or, by arrangement, from the police station).

In cases where recovered property has been taken to the offices of the insurance company, you can call there to have a look at it and say if you wish to have it back.

As a rule, insurers do not want recovered articles: the goods have to be stored and sold by auction and are quite likely to make a loss. Insurers would sooner sell them to a ready buyer – the previous owner. If an article is recovered intact and you want it back, the whole of the amount paid to you for it has to be repaid to the insurers. If an article is returned damaged, you need pay back only part of the money received for it. Do not necessarily agree to the first figure asked: it may pay to make a counter-offer.

reviewing your insurance cover
After a burglary, you should
- make sure that the sum insured for your contents is up to date, taking account of items stolen and replaced
- take note of any limits in the policy so that you can specify high value items which exceed the individual item limit
- if necessary, raise the limit on unspecified 'valuables' (this may mean paying an additional premium to increase the percentage of total sum insured or the specified figure)
- decide if you wish to change the basis of your policy – for instance, from indemnity to replacement-as-new – or to pay the extra premium for all-risks cover.

When you buy a replacement for a valuable item, keep the receipt and, for jewellery, get a valuation 'for insurance purposes' from the jeweller. (This is free at the time of buying, but if you take jewellery or other valuables to be valued at any other time, you will be charged a fee based on the value of the items.) Tell the insurers, so that the item can be covered straightaway.

Mark your new possessions, wherever possible, with some identifying symbol or your postcode; take a photograph of any small valuables, such as jewellery, that cannot easily be marked.

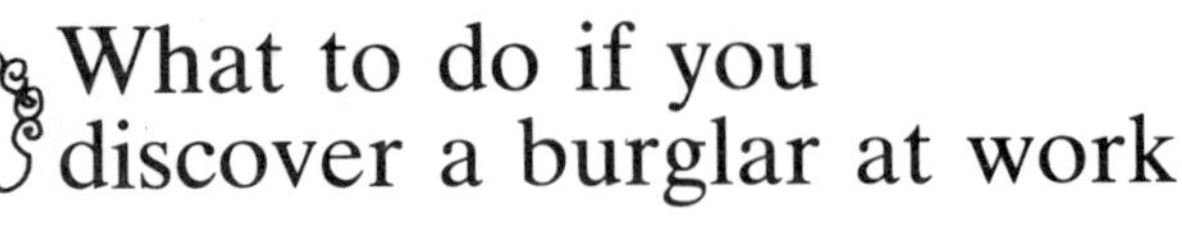

What to do if you discover a burglar at work

If you wake in the night and realise that there is an intruder in the house or flat, try to get to the telephone to call the police without his knowing that you are awake and taking action. But you may not be able to do so without being heard or seen, in which case it would be better to disturb him by turning on lights or making a noise and let him escape. Try to get a look at him as he goes and watch to see in which direction he makes off. Call the police at once and let them know what you have seen.

If you return home and realise that a burglar either is, or has been, in your home (at this point, you are not sure which), do not go in. If he is no longer inside, you do not lose any more by waiting for the police. If he is, the burglar may have a worked-out plan of what he is going to do if somebody comes in and may be prepared to use force, perhaps using a jemmy as a weapon.

You may walk in not realising that there is a burglar in the house. There is a chance that the opportunist type of intruder, who is usually more scared than you are, will drop the goods and make off quickly once you disturb him. But if he does not, and confronts you, do not be heroic about challenging him – better to get away as quickly as you can.

If you arrive at your home and realise that a burglar is at work and you manage not to disturb him, there are two possible courses of action, and you must make an immediate decision.

The courses of action open to you are to
- enter the house and, if the burglar is there, try to detain him, and call the police
- go to a neighbour's house or nearby telephone box, call the police, and wait for them.

Unless you are big enough and fit enough and young enough and strong enough to tackle a burglar with a reasonable chance of success, the categoric advice is not to try. Go away quickly and quietly and telephone the police. They are the professionals who are trained to deal with these situations.

Use 999 or the local police emergency number and give your address clearly, with specific directions on how to get there if required. Tell the police the location of any back entrance or side door so that they can cover that area. Then wait for the police to arrive.

Even if more than one person returns home to find intruders, do not enter or challenge. Leave one person to watch while the other telephones the police from a neighbouring telephone. Do nothing to let the intruders know that they have been observed.

Wait a discreet distance away, to signal to the police on their arrival.

Make good use of the time until the police arrive. Look along the road and note any unusual cars that are parked: a strange car with a warm engine may belong to the burglars. Make a descriptive note of a car as full as possible, with make and colour as well as registration number – the description is important because the number could be false but the car may later be stopped by police on the description.

If the burglar leaves before the police arrive, note the details of the vehicle he goes into or off in, and take as good a description of him as possible. He is unlikely to be wearing a cloth cap and a striped jersey or to carry a bag over his shoulder marked "swag"; in fact, he will closely resemble any ordinary citizen.

You should note sex, height, approximate weight, build, colour of hair, whether bearded or clean shaven (if a man), complexion, shape of face, size and shape of nose, if wearing spectacles, style of hairdressing, peculiarities of walk, and mode of dress.

Remember that if he is subsequently arrested, you may be called upon to attend an identity parade to pick him out from a line-up of people of similar appearance, so make sure that you have as good a mental picture of him as possible.

If the burglar gets away before the arrival of the police, and you enter the house, remember not to touch things until the police have come and had a chance to dust for fingerprints. If articles are dropped by a fleeing intruder, do not touch them, and do not touch anything in the house until everything has been fully examined by the police.

If a lone burglar emerges before the police arrive and there are several young athletic males (rugger players) present, they might consider tackling the intruder, but always remember that there is a possibility that he may be armed. If your burglar is armed, with a gun, knife or anything, then let him go. Your property can be replaced but you have only one life – lose it, and it is gone for ever.

Someone who gets injured through a crime of violence or as a result of going to the aid of the police or of another member of the public, can claim compensation (a lump sum) through the criminal injuries compensation scheme.

Details of the scheme and an application form with notes on the information required can be obtained from the Criminal Injuries Compensation Board, 10–12 Russell Square, London WC1B 5EN. An application must be made within 3 years of the date of injury and you must agree to authorise the board to get information from doctors, dentists, police, employer. You can apply even if the assailant/burglar is not known or has not been apprehended.

INDEX

Avoiding back trouble

explains how the spine is constructed and how not to stress it in everyday activities such as housework, driving, lifting and carrying, gardening, sitting. It describes symptoms of back trouble and advises on how to cope with an acute attack of back pain. It tells what to expect when examined by specialists (including the diagnostic terms that may be used) and the treatments that may be prescribed. The book ends with suggestions about how to avoid becoming a chronic back sufferer.

Avoiding heart trouble

identifies the factors which make a person more likely to develop heart trouble and describes how the various risk factors interact: cigarette smoking, raised blood pressure, high level of blood fats, stress, hereditary and dietary factors, oral contraceptives, overweight. It warns of the more serious signs and symptoms of heart trouble and, where possible, tells you what can be done about them.

Central heating

will help you to weigh up the alternative methods of heating your home. It discusses the factors you should consider when choosing the fuel, with charts of relative running costs. Finding an efficient installer, and dealing with him, are covered in detail, and so are the merits of various types of insulation. There is information, and illustrations, on all the equipment involved – boilers, radiators, circulation systems and methods of control. The book also gives advice on problems that might occur after installation.

Cutting your cost of living

suggests ways of spending less money without changing your standard of living. The book includes ideas on how to reduce your bills for food, toiletries, heating and holidays. There is a section on managing your money, and practical advice is given on growing your own fruit and vegetables, and on what jobs it is worth doing yourself.

Earning money at home

for anyone who wants or needs to take up an activity at home that will bring some extra (or essential) cash, this book sets out what is entailed. It puts forward the pros and cons of working at home, stressing the self-discipline required and the reorganisation that may be necessary. The statutory requirements about planning permission, liability for insurance, national insurance and tax are all explained. Advertising and getting work, costing and charging for it, getting supplies, keeping accounts, are all important factors that are fully covered. The second section of the book suggests some types of work that might be suitable, with or without previous experience, giving a brief account of what may be involved in undertaking them. Courses for brushing up a skill or hobby to a more professional standard are suggested, and sources of further help and advice are given. The final section discusses what to do if your venture fares badly and, more optimistically, how to expand the business when successful.

Extending your house

describes what is involved in having an extension built on to a house or bungalow. The book is a step-by-step account of what has to be done, when and by whom. It deals with drawing a sketch plan, con-sulting an architect or other professional consultant, contacting a builder, arranging a contract and getting quotations. It explains how the Building Regulations affect the position and design of an extension, and how to apply to the local authority for planning permission and Building Regulations approval. For the technically-minded, various aspects of construction work are described. There is a glossary and many explanatory drawings.

Getting a new job

is a practical guide to the steps to take from when one job ends to the day the next one begins. The circumstances relating to unfair dismissal are explained, as are the remedies available. The book defines redundancy and lists your rights; it explains how redundancy payment is calculated and what can be done when an employer does not pay up. It also suggests how an employer can help a redundant employee find another job.

The book deals with job hunting, how to apply, what to do to get an interview and making sure that the interview goes well. It covers the points to consider when being offered a job and what is involved as an employee, including the legal rights and obligations on both sides.

The legal side of buying a house

for buying an owner-occupied house in England or Wales, this book will guide you step by step through the legal procedure. It explains what is involved and follows in detail the whole process of doing your own conveyancing – from placing a deposit, obtaining all the relevant forms and filling them in, dealing with the Land Registry and local authority, to exchange of contracts and, finally, completion. Even if you have decided that doing your own conveyancing would be too time-consuming or difficult for you, this book will help you check what your solicitor is doing at each stage. The book also deals with the legally less complicated procedure of selling your house.

Living through middle age

faces up to the changes that this stage of life may bring, whether inevitable (in skin, hair, eyes, teeth) or avoidable, such as being overweight, smoking or drinking too much, insomnia. It discusses the symptoms and treatment of specific disorders that are fairly common in men and women over 40, and for women the effects of the menopause and gynaecological problems. Psychological difficulties for both men and women are discussed, and the possible need for sexual adjustment. Throughout, practical advice is given on overcoming problems that may arise.

The newborn baby

concentrates on the health and welfare of a new baby and reassures the mother about what is usual and normal in a baby's development. It deals primarily with the first weeks after the baby is born but there is also plenty of information about feeding and development in the following weeks and months. There are sections dealing with problems such as prematurity and the rhesus factor and descriptions of routine tests. There is advice about when to seek help from midwife, health visitor, clinic doctor or general practitioner.

On getting divorced

explains the procedure for getting a divorce in England or Wales, and how, in a straightforward undefended case, it can be done by the postal procedure. The legal advice scheme and other state help for someone with a low income is described and there is advice on coping in reduced circumstances. Calculations for maintenance and division of property are given, with details of the orders the court may make for financial settlements between the divorcing couple and for arrangements about the children.

Pregnancy month by month

tells in details what a pregnant woman can expect at each stage of antenatal care. The book discusses where to have a baby, and compares hospital, GP maternity unit, nursing home and home confinement. It gives reasons for the various tests and examinations at antenatal clinics, and tells how to deal with the minor ailments that often accompany pregnancy. Sections on genetic counselling, having twins, claiming maternity benefits, fertility problems, contraception, abortion and provisions for unmarried mothers are also included.

Raising the money to buy your home

explains the choice of mortgage and lender that faces you when needing a loan to buy your first or a new home. It deals with building societies, banks, local authorities, insurance companies, warning about the limitations and conditions that each may impose. The book describes how interest rates can vary and shows, with tables, the difference between the quoted interest rate and what you actually pay. There are also calculations to enable you to work out your own payments on a repayment mortgage. The book takes you through the steps of applying for a loan, and deals with what happens if you have difficulty with keeping up the payments or want to pay off your mortgage.

What to do when someone dies

explains about doctors' certificates, about deaths reported to the coroner and what this entails, about registering a death and getting the various certificates that may be needed afterwards. Differences between burial and cremation procedure are discussed, and the arrangements that have to be made, mainly through the undertaker, for the funeral. The book details the various national insurance benefits that may be claimed.

Where to live after retirement

tackles the difficult subject of a suitable place to live in old age. The book offers practical advice on the decision whether to move or to stay put and adapt the present home to be easier to live in. It weighs up the pros and cons of the alternatives open to an older person, and the financial aspects involved, considers sheltered housing and granny flats, the problems of living in someone else's household, and residential homes.

Which? way to buy, sell and move house

takes you through all the stages of moving to another home – considering the pros and cons of different places, house hunting, viewing, having a survey, making an offer, getting a mortgage, completing the purchase, selling the present home. It explains the legal procedures and the likely costs. Buying and selling at an auction and in Scotland are specifically dealt with. The practical arrangements for the move and for any repairs or improvements to the new house are described.

Advice is given for easing the tasks of sorting, packing and moving possessions, people and pets, with a removal firm or by doing it yourself, and for making the day of the move go smoothly.

Which? way to slim

is the complete guide to losing weight and staying slim. The book separates fact from fallacy, and gives a balanced view of essentials such as suitable weight ranges, target weights, exercise, and the advantages and disadvantages of different methods of dieting. The book highlights the dangers of being overweight and warns of the risks in middle age, during pregnancy, when giving up smoking. Every aspect of slimming is appraised – from appetite suppressants to yoga.

There are also sections on slimmers' cookery, foods and aids for slimmers, eating out, slimming groups, help from doctors, the psychology of slimming, activity and exercise. Tables of Calorie and carbohydrate values of foods and drinks are provided for easy day-to-day reference.

Wills and probate

is a book about wills and how to make them, and about the administration of an estate undertaken by executors without the help of a solicitor. One section deals with intestacy and explains the difficulties which can arise when there is no will. *Wills and probate* goes step by step through the tasks of an executor concerned with a straightforward will: reading the will, the valuation of the estate, payment of tax, the steps involved in obtaining probate, the distribution of the estate in accordance with the will, the transfer of property to the new owner, and explains clearly the procedures involved at every stage. The book also shows how to make a will – prepare it, sign it and have it witnessed.

The Which? book of do-it-yourself

tells – and shows – you how to take advantage of the clever devices and labour-saving materials on the market, how to do yourself the hundred-and-one jobs around the home and garden that it costs so much to have done by a tradesman. It includes sections on electricity; extensions; insulation; painting; plumbing; floors and doors; roofs and chimneys; wallpapers and windows.

With this book, you can do the job for the cost of materials and tools alone – adding to the value of your home, making it safer and more comfortable to live in – and enjoying the satisfaction of doing a good job, yourself.

The Which? book of house plants

is a practical guide to choosing, buying and caring for your house plants. The plants are arranged alphabetically in groups of plant types. It deals with shopping; tools and equipment; composts and soils; pots and containers; general care; light; position; heat and humidity; watering and feeding; propagation; keeping plants healthy.

The Which? guide to your rights

will help protect you, as well as inform you, against being taken advantage of by, say, the police who stop you for speeding, or your local education authority who insist on a certain school for your child. It deals with the legal aspects of health and education, rates and taxes, social services and benefits and a person's rights as a consumer.

The Which? heritage guide

is a guide to places worth visiting in Britain, from castles to stately homes to modest cottages, all with their own special merits. Also included are galleries and gardens, monuments and museums. The entries give a brief summary of a place – its history, origins, style, surroundings and special features – in such a way that it makes it easy for you to assess whether it is the sort of place you would enjoy. Each entry gives extensive, useful information on the facilities available: catering, picnic areas, shops, facilities for the disabled, where dogs are allowed, group reductions, cost of entry, phone number, car parking, how to find the place, and opening times.

Which? way to repair and restore furniture

is a practical guide with step-by-step diagrams. It covers restoration techniques – identifying wood, stripping off dirt and old polish, repairing joints, letting in new wood and disguising your repair, putting back the surface finish and colour, repairing surfaces of leather and veneer, and repairing metalwork. It covers upholstery, starting with a simple drop-in chair seat and progressing to more complex springing and upholstery techniques. The book covers specific repairs to various types of chairs and tables, and larger furniture like chests of drawers and desks. It gives hints on what tools to buy and how to look after them.

Which? way to run your car

is a practical, commonsense guide to car ownership. It includes sections on buying new or secondhand; getting good value; raising the money; improving your car; insurance; routine maintenance; saving petrol; straightforward repairs; going abroad; learning to drive; accidents.

All these publications are available from
Consumers' Association, Caxton Hill, Hertford SG13 7LZ
and from booksellers.